BITE ME

BITE ME

TELL-ALL TALES OF AN EMERGENCY VETERINARIAN

Laura C Lefkowitz, DVM

Book design by Maureen Cutajar
www.gopublished.com

DISCLAIMER

I have tried to recreate events and conversations from my memories of them. In order to maintain their anonymity I have changed the names of individuals and places. In some cases I have compressed events; in others I have made two people into one. I may have changed identifying characteristics and details such as physical properties, timelines and places of occurrence. Everything here is true, but it may not be entirely factual.

To my family of friends who have cheered me on through both the good times and the bad times.
I am eternally grateful.

CONTENTS

I knew that if I allowed fear to overtake me, my journey was doomed. Fear, to a great extent, is born of a story we tell ourselves, and so I chose to tell myself a different story from the one women are told. I decided I was safe. I was strong. I was brave.

—Cheryl Strayed

INTRODUCTION

I have been a veterinarian for more than twenty years and during that time I believe I have examined several thousand animals and have had some form of communication with at least that many owners. And after all of these years I still find that on a daily basis veterinary medicine continues to surprise me, humble me, enlighten me, devastate me, educate me, enrage me and elevate me. One thing is for sure about my job, being a veterinarian means that every day that I am practicing my trade I am truly alive.

My job is never boring. A day does not go by when I do not see a medical problem whose cause I cannot determine, or see an old medical problem that has a new symptom or a different outcome than what I expected. Never a day within a month's time when I don't have to look up the meaning of a medical word I have never seen, or research a dose or side effect of a medication, or relearn the name of an obscure part of an animal's anatomy, or have the need to search out the husbandry or medical treatment of a semi-exotic species that arrived through my door. There is never a week that I don't see a trauma or a type of toxicity or an unfortunate circumstance to an animal which I have never seen before. There is rarely a day when a client doesn't make me laugh, or make me angry, or frustrate me to no end, Or that I do not receive a friendly nuzzle from one patient, have another one turn and snap at me, and have yet another one fearfully glare at me from its position in the corner behind its owner. It is unusual to have a day when I don't feel helpless in my ability to help my patient or to help the owner of my patient. And thankfully, there is never a day that I don't feel cocky about my abilities to heal or fix an animal because I have seen and successfully treated that condition hundreds of times before.

I have been writing this book since I started veterinary school. I have spent my entire career jotting down the details of my daily encounters as a veterinarian that at the time seemed notable. As is the case with most people who work within the walls of a veterinary hospital, I repeatedly find myself in the midst of the dramas and traumas and tragedies of my patients and their families. My daily work can also involve doing some of the most vile and disgusting things imaginable, things that I am usually hoping that no one that I know well will ever find out about. All of this sickly fascinating material provides ripe fodder for an aspiring writer who, in this case, just happens to be me. In the midst of my stories that take place within the walls of a veterinary hospital, I have intermixed the stories of the medical encounters which I have had with animals and their owners during my travels through third-world countries. These were all jotted down in battered journals that now reside, stacked in a wicker basket, in my closet. These memories seemed important to the whole tale, as my travel experiences profoundly influenced my medical philosophies and the approach that I take when I am presented with animals whose owners have no limit to what they will spend on their pet or when, conversely, I am faced with a family who has no spare income for an animal who they dearly love.

When I read books or magazines about veterinarians, most of them tell cute and heartwarming tales of what our days our like. TV shows and movies seemed to be filled with images and story lines of the fairy tale, fun-filled lives of veterinarians. These forums tend to depict veterinarian's days as being filled with cute fuzzy puppies, benign medical conditions, routine vaccinations and animals who sustain nothing more than a small laceration or an easily repaired broken leg after being involved in a trauma. They also tend to show smiling clients who irrefutably care for their pets and who will pay for any recommended treatment that the veterinarian makes. At some point I realized that these media versions of my job are incongruous with the daily realities that I experience. My stories don't shy away from the harsh realities of veterinary medicine. They include the dirty, gritty, funny, sad, frightening, gross, reality version of veterinary medicine. I wanted animal lovers, pet owners, aspiring children and students entering the veterinary profession to understand what really happens within a veterinary hospital. I also wanted the reader to be immersed into the conversations that veterinarians are having with their clients as well as surreptitiously overhear the conversations that the veterinarians are having within the privacy of their own minds.

My original intent was to entertain people with the myriad of amusing and fascinating stories I have experienced over the years. A secondary goal was to softly educate people about the more common diseases and traumas and toxicities that occur so frequently to animals in the hopes that owners may be able to avoid these common mistakes with their own pets. But overtime my hopes for this book have changed a bit, particularly when I started to recognize the plight of my profession. Veterinarians have recently been identified as being at the top of a list of professionals who are most likely to commit suicide.[1,2] This statistic first stunned me, then saddened me, and then made me profoundly angry when I thought about how much compassion, care, time, and personal sacrifice that my colleagues put into their work while caring for sick animals and distressed owners every day. We are a profession that is trying as a whole to do good for others yet, it seems, we are not very good at caring for ourselves. This statistic probably surprises the average person who is accustomed to their own perception of veterinarians as

---

[1] Bartram DJ, Baldwin DS, Veterinary surgeons and suicide. A structural review of possible influences on increased risk. Vet Rec 2010;166(15);451
[2] Nett RJ, Witte TK, Holzbauer SM, et al, Notes from the field prevalence of suicide risks among veterinarians-United State. 2014, Morb Mortal Wkly Rep 2-15,64{6};149

people who spend their days snuggling with frisky, cute kittens and roly-poly puppies. To them there is no rational reason why our jobs should be so stressful. Yet, my guess is that this statistic is not nearly as surprising to anyone who has actually worked within the animal care industry.

As this unpleasant conversation starts to unfold, mostly in the arena of veterinary forums and journals, I realized that one of the main reasons that I wanted my stories to express the realism of the profession was so that people could better understand the hardships and stresses and frustrations and inadequacies that exist in my field and amongst my colleagues. I want them to see how veterinarians, who are not given any special training in grief or trauma counseling, deal with extreme emotions and situations at a frequency and intensity that few other professions in the world ever have to do. I wanted people to vicariously live in the world that I live in and then come to their own conclusions about why veterinarians have hit the top of a list that no profession wants to be on. My hopes are that with better public recognition of how difficult of a profession veterinary medicine can be, it will create a network of support which may help veterinary professionals to climb out of the hole that we have found ourselves in.

As I sit at my computer I find myself trying not to disturb the tiny feathered form of an abandoned duckling that is now nested in the upper right corner of my keyboard. My technicians promptly handed the little thing over to me when it arrived at our hospital, giving me motherly, nurse-like instructions on how to keep it warm. I accomplish this critical task of countering hypothermia by allowing the duckling to snuggle down deep into the folds of my clothing. Its current position on my keyboard, now that it is fully warmed, is physical evidence of the obscure situations that I often find myself immersed in while trying to perform my routine duties of being an ER veterinarian. Seemingly this profession redefines routine. Truly, how many other professionals have to cope with the indignity of an overly feisty, now somewhat cantankerous, duckling hissing and shaking its tail feathers at them every time they try to type the letter "P" while at work? On the bright side, I know intuitively that it is these unique, heartwarming, and fuzzy-type moments which are not in the average office job's description which make my job so appealing. It is a big part of why so many young people are clamoring to become members of this profession. The reality version of the moment quickly emerges as I watch a drop of liquid poo seep downward and then westward on my keyboard. As I frantically try to stop the green flow from progressing and simultaneously attempt to shoo the very persistent duckling away from my keyboard, I try hard to recreate that warm fuzzy feeling that only moments before I had been basking in, but it is rapidly dissipating away. Just smile and cherish the moment, is what I finally tell myself, because if my past shifts at this ER hospital are a good indicator, then very shortly there will be bigger calamities to worry about.

I hope that my stories will make you laugh, cry, become enraged, and feel more enlightened in regards to the world of veterinary medicine, for these are the effects that these stories still have on me.

Laura Lefkowitz, DVM

CHAPTER I

NIGHT OF TRAUMAS

Summer is the busy season in the veterinary ER business. Dogs and cats are fighting, animals are bolting in front of cars, and garbage cans are being knocked over and their contents scavenged. Grass awns are finding their way into our animals' eyes and ears. Owners are camping with their dogs who are drinking stagnant water, eating poisonous mushrooms, and riding loose in truck beds. Hunting dogs are nosing up to venomous snakes, or cornering sharp-toothed animals, or overheating in the excitement of the chase. Disease-carrying ticks, mosquitoes, and fleas are biting through the protective fur of animals' coats. Unvaccinated puppies are sniffing virus-laden feces in the park. Cats are scrapping over their territories and arriving at our hospital with nasty wounds on their bodies. Every summer the veterinary business booms.

Emergencies have a tendency to show up in groups. One evening I admitted two dogs with severe traumatic injuries to their eyes. They were admitted for consultations with our ophthalmologist and I spent the night wondering which one's cornea might rupture first. The next night toxicities were the menu du jour and I treated three separate dogs for the inappropriate substances that they had eaten. The following week two dogs who were in fulminant heart failure stared at each other through the glass doors of the oxygen chambers, each in a sad contest to breathe and to survive. Some nights it is the type of owner that shows up in groups. One evening, I may see a never ending array of ornery owners who won't do anything for their pets and on the next evening, I cannot convince owners to take their minimally ill animal home.

One sweaty evening in July I dubbed as 'The Night of Traumas.' Unrelentingly, animals arrived through my doors beaten up by different types of trauma. By the end of the evening I had assembled an array of bruised and battered animals who were each fighting for their lives in different manners. I had prayed for a quiet evening as I drove into work that night, for my third evening in a row, but as it turns out the Gods of the Emergency Room were laughing at me instead of empathizing with me.

I arrived to find that I was short one technician who was out ill and the others on duty were cranky and exhausted from the preceding busy nights. Several semi-critical patients had already been admitted to the ER. One was an elderly farm cat who had not moved quickly enough away from the hay thrasher and, as a result, the lower portion of his leg had been left behind in the farmer's field, cleanly cut off at the knee. A dachshund named Ellie, who earlier that day had been hit by a car, was housed in a lower cage by our treatment table. X-rays had shown multiple pelvic fractures that left her unable to use her hind legs. She also had some large wounds which necessitated frequent bandage changes, as the bandages that covered the wounds were rapidly saturating with bloody fluid. The problem with treating Ellie was that she was an unsocialized, snapping, screaming fury of a dog. Even without full use of her hind legs she still had the capacity to lunge forward and snap into the air in an attempt to maim us. Simply getting Ellie out of the cage required throwing a blanket over her head and wrapping her in a bundle, like we would with a feral cat, so that no one would get hurt by her gnashing teeth. The mere act of walking close to her cage would start Ellie incessantly screaming and howling until we were all crazed from the sound. No amount of kind soothing or admonishments or increasing doses of pain medications made any difference to the amount of noise that Ellie made. Her vocalizations had nothing to do with pain but were a reflection of her fearful and unsocialized temperament.

By 11:00 p.m. the proverbial crap had hit the fan so hard that it was being winged around our hospital, smearing the walls as it spun. Every exam room was full and I had a lobby full of people holding various species and sizes of animals all with distressed and impatient looks on their faces. I was in a room examining a patient when a technician popped in and asked me to evaluate an incoming critical patient. It was a cat named Chica. Chica had been lazily sleeping in her own back yard when two dogs grabbed her from opposite ends and pulled her in a vicious form of tug of war. The owners saw her escape from the dogs grip and then walk back into the garage. Foolishly deciding that if she was able to walk she must be okay, they left her in their garage to sleep. Three hours later they brought her into our hospital unconscious and cold. Animal attacks are some of the worst injuries that we see in a veterinary hospital. Big animals have the tendency to grab and shake little animals, with the end result often being a spinal fractures. And external wounds sustained from a fight are often deceptively minor compared to the internal injuries that are created.

Chica was panting with pain and her hair was matted down with saliva. I treated her for shock and performed the additional diagnostics necessary to insure that none of her internal organs had been ruptured by a penetrating tooth. Chica's skin was badly bruised all over and air had seeped out under her skin, giving it a bubble wrap-like feeling. This gave me a clue that an air-containing structure such as her trachea or lungs had been pierced. I hoped that we could save her.

I counselled the crying family of four in the room. If she lived through the shock and didn't need a major surgery to repair a ruptured intestine or a torn diaphragm, or if her lungs weren't torn, or if she didn't throw clots to her organs, or if she didn't end up with an overwhelming infection of her body, then she may live. I brought up the difficult subject of the expenses involved and informed them that she may still die despite everything that we would do. I was aware that none of this sounded good. I was not trying to dissuade them from treating her. I very much wanted them to treat her and give her the chance to live, but it was equally as important that they fully understood the potential outcomes of her trauma. If they chose to proceed there were no guarantees. In medicine none of us know with one hundred percent clarity who is going to do well and who is not. I wished that I had the fabled crystal ball to foresee her future, as possessing one would make my job so much easier.

As I spoke to them, I watched the husband and wife, trying to gauge their reactions to my words. I was not insensitive to the fact that there was a nine-year-old and a fourteen-year-old in the room tearfully sobbing. The parents were exchanging, "Can we really afford this," intermixed with the "We have to do it for the sake of the children," glances at each other. And the children were shooting the "I am never going to speak to you again if you don't help our cat," look at their parents. The dynamics of a distraught family in an emergency situation are draining. I felt for everyone involved. I felt for the poor cat who'd just been violently traumatized in what was just a game between two overly-exuberant dogs. I felt for the parents who had a home to support and children to feed. I felt for the children who had grown up with this cat, loved her dearly and who could not imagine their lives without her.

"I'll give you time to think about it," I told them, stepping out to check on their cat while they hashed out amongst themselves what was the right thing to do for their kitty. They also needed to decide what was the right thing for their family. I didn't have the time or the energy to get in the midst of these emotions on such a busy night. Right then the family crisis was a distraction from my job, which at that moment was to treat their cat and the other hospitalized patients to the best of my ability.

I continued on with the outpatient clients that kept trickling in. The board remained filled with the names of people and pets who were waiting in the seven exam rooms. In between rooms, I sneaked back to reevaluate my patients. Every time I passed the cage of the dachshund, Ellie, she screamed out and lunged at the bars of the cage with her teeth bared. And each time this occurred, I jumped at the unexpected assault, the piercing noise setting off a sharp pang in my head which resonated down my spine. My legs ached and I started to get that overwhelmed feeling. I reached for my bottle of No-Doze and sipped down the bitter tasting pills with black coffee, triple the caffeine to keep me going through what I could tell was going to be an agonizingly long night.

The family with the torn-apart cat stepped out to tell me they wanted to give their kitty a chance. I was glad for the cat and composed a treatment plan for twenty-four hours of care. She was so severely injured that I thought it best to plan in short intervals, as things could change rapidly. In room three, a distraught man kept peeking out the door to see how long it was going to be until I saw his dog who he believed had a fatal ear infection. Down the hall I could hear a woman complaining to my technician about our prices and about the wait. From room seven, I could still hear the sobbing from where I had left a women after euthanizing her canine companion of fourteen years. My technicians were frantically running around admitting animals, treating in-house patients and appeasing clients. It was a mad house, a zoo, a frantic frenzy of stress that was seeping the energy out of everyone who was working that night.

"I just got a call from a woman who said she's bringing her dog down whose head has been chopped partially off. She doesn't know if he's going to make it here," the technician told me. "They are two hours away."

Great, I thought, imagining that injury in my head and, given the chaos of the evening, was not sure if I would be happy or sad if he made it. It didn't sound like a promising injury and either way it would likely be a bad outcome for that poor fellow.

I continued with the incoming patients, closing up small lacerations, rinsing the mouth of a dog who chewed up a battery, treating a poodle's back pain and fielding phone calls from owners who were checking in on their hospitalized pets. In the midst of it my boyfriend called, frantic because our poodle had broken its toenail and was bleeding small spots of blood all over our house.

"Just stuff the nail with flour and put a wrap on it. It will be fine," I told him, practically hanging up the phone as I spit out the words. I'm sure the irritability was audible in my voice. I didn't want to deal with the non-emergency dramas of my own family on this particular night.

In the oxygen cage, my canine patient who sustained lung trauma after being hit by a car several days ago was persisting in his slow struggle to recover and breathe. His anxious owner insisted on sitting with him for hours on end. This in itself is not unusual, but intermittently the owner jumped up to harass me with needy, energy sucking questions.

She spotted me and rushed over to ask, "When is the last time the barolyme has been changed in the oxygen cage?" I only had a short interval of time to fill out treatment orders for an incoming pet.

"I'll have one of my technicians check on that," I told her doing my best to give her the amount of attention she required while simultaneously attempting to escape. She knew perfectly well that I wasn't the person who would know when the oxygen cage's barolyme had been changed.

When there was a pause in the momentum, I stopped at the computer to write up a chart. I was trying to keep the growing pile in my box at bay. We are expected to have the records ready by morning so the family veterinarians who receive them are appeased that we are not forgetting about them. Around one in the morning, just as I was thinking that things were starting to quiet down, and that I may actually be able to catch up, eat something and temporarily recover from the mounting stress, I heard the dooming sound of the after-hours door bell. This sound, in the middle of the night, is usually a forewarning of the arrival of some dying or critical animal.

"The dog with his head chopped off is here," announced the secretary over the intercom. She was speaking in a monotone voice as if she was reporting the evening weather.

Even I, a seasoned veterinarian with more than 18 years experience, was shocked by the appearance of the little dog that was carried into the back by my worried technician. The dog was sitting up and at first glance, when viewing her from the right side, she looked relatively normal. But when my gaze moved up and over her eyes, the sight quickly became repulsive. The dog had a laceration which began over her right eye and extended across the top of her left eye, down her face and across the base of her left ear. The skin on her head was, in essence, peeled from her skull and was hanging over backwards in the direction of her tail. In an odd peek-a-boo fashion her entire skull bone was exposed. I could see the muscles and the round shape of her left eye ball, which moved around in her skull in puppet-like fashion. Her left ear was cut straight through the canal and half of it was peeled back. A perfect circular opening was visible exposing her ear drum for close inspection. The movie, "Face Off" came to mind…a film where two people change identities by surgically switching the skin off their faces.

"Feisty" was looking around, a bit distraught about being in a strange environment, but otherwise without any major concerns that the top of her head was peeled off backwards. I didn't have the slightest idea of what could have caused this type of laceration.

'Give her some hydro," I told my technicians, giving them permission to dope away her pain with opioids. Then I walked into the room where the owners were waiting. I knew this was going to be an interesting conversation. My first assessment identified them as hillbillies. *Don't judge a book by its cover*, my grandmother Sally's wise words sharply floated through my head. But this book cover was ragged and torn and looked like it had been under the garbage heap for a few years. It was hard not to judge it.

"It was a cougar,' the woman drawled at me. "Saw her foot prints in our garden. Feisty here went after her. We came all the way down from the mountains. We live far out in the woods."

The woman was middle-aged and overweight and wearing a stained, flowered t-shirt. Her hair was frizzy and partially braided. The man was in dirty jeans and a tattered, plaid shirt. He smelled of smoke and seemed to be smeared with grease. He was missing several teeth and, with my brief inspection, the rest of them did not look very healthy either.

"Feisty has lost most of the skin on the top of her head. We need to try to flip it back over and sew it back on and see if the skin will survive," I informed the owners. "This injury is so bad that it would be best if it was done by our boarded surgeons." I said this knowing that it was unlikely that they could afford that option, but sometimes people surprise you. I was truly hoping that we could help Feisty. Actually, I was truly hoping they would pick the surgeon choice as I was not looking forward to trying to fix that.

They quickly confirmed that the care I suggested was not affordable. I then went through the painfully slow process of trying to figure out what treatment options they could afford for their dog. I knew that half-best care may not be good enough for Feisty. In a situation such as this, less than optimum medical care may result in failure of the treatment. I offered various treatment plans and varying standards of care, all of which they shook their heads at and declined. With each new estimate they told me that they were unable to afford it. It's not that they didn't care, it was obvious to me that they truly loved Feisty, it was simply that they couldn't afford the care that she needed.

"Just bandage it," they told me, "and we'll bring her to our farm vet in the morning."

I knew that would be a mistake for their dog but I was out of op tions. Her healing would require extensive treatments and I could not give away our services for free.

I pulled Feisty's face back into place so that all of her facial features lined up. Surprisingly she looked quite good. I tacked a few sutures around in a circular fashion, to keep the skin in place. It was hard to tell that there was a problem except for the thin sliver of tissue sticking out around the circumference of the laceration. I knew it was only a temporary illusion and that the real repair was going to be a difficult one, requiring extended care for the dog and the owners. If the skin flap didn't live, Feisty would be a goner. Gratuitously, I gave Feisty an injection of antibiotics, an injection of pain medications, and placed a bandage around her head. I handed the now more pleasant appearing Feisty back to her owner.

"Best of luck in getting Feistys' face fixed," I said. There was something innately weird about that statement.

After reluctantly sending Feisty back with her owners, I settled in to finish my duties. The incoming rooms had stopped. I started to examine the charts of my hospitalized patients to see if any changes needed to be made in their treatment plans. When that was finished, I started the arduous task of completing records. It was 6:00 am. I was home free. In one hour the interns would arrive to examine their hospitalized patients. Rounds would begin at 8:00 a.m. and last for about one hour and only then would my patients and responsibilities would be transferred to the incoming day staff. I was beat to crap, exhausted and cranky.

The dreaded doorbell rang again. I collapsed my head onto the desk. I still had to reexamine my overnight patients before morning rounds, change the bandages on the out-of-control, screaming dachshund, make up discharges for patients that were leaving, call one referring vet about an animal that I was transferring back to him, and finish my charts. I didn't have time to see yet another patient.

The arriving Chihuahua was a long time patient of one of our surgeons, and had had several surgeries in the past. The owner is a good client, but one who requires extra TLC. Jack, their Chihuahua was here because he had been lame on his leg for two days.

"Why at 6:00 a.m., and why today, and why on emergency?" I practically screamed at my equally frazzled technician.

My stress levels were boiling over. I suddenly felt angry that the hospital wasn't providing us with more help in the mornings. I had a hundred things left to do before I could leave, and the emergencies kept coming in and I didn't have enough staff. I was composing my pissed off letter to the hospital manager in my head as I went into the room.

This dog was going to need sedation and x-rays and the owner needed to have a large amount of patience. As well as checking out his lameness the owner wanted me to examine several lumps which had been growing slowly over the last five months. I was silently screaming in my head, but the perfect smile remained on my face as I patiently examined Jack and did a needle aspirate of his lumps. While I was looking at the slides, the doorbell rang again. *Bring it on,* I resignedly thought to myself. I placed Jack above Ellie, the dachshund who shrieked and screamed mercilessly. Jack appeared perplexed and unhappy with the chaos of his new surroundings.

The incoming patient was a large Malamute who had been shot by its neighbor. Welcome to the rural Pacific Northwest. The owner who brought him in pointed to a gaping hole about one centimeter wide on his dog's side. By how vibrant the dog looked, I guessed that the ammunition didn't hit any major vessels otherwise he would never have made it to our ER room. The dog's gum color was a bit pale and I was still worried that he had experienced an internal bleed which had temporarily stopped.

"When I tried to clean it with peroxide the wound sucked in air," the owner informed me.

Well, that's not an encouraging sign, I thought to myself. That's a strong suggestion that the offending bullet penetrated the thorax and his lungs.

He went on to tell me in an emotionless voice, "At first he seemed kind of lazy but now he's okay."

I walked back into the room where Jack's owners resided and felt relieved to be honestly able to tell them that I had to attend to a dog who was shot in the chest. This emergency seemed sufficiently valid for them

15

to accept that Jack's care could be left for later. Great, one less patient that I needed to worry about at that moment.

I returned to the gun-shot Malamute. I composed an estimate of what we needed to do for this dog: x-rays of his chest, an ultrasound to insure the bullet's path hadn't ripped through his abdomen, get an IV line and fluids running, administer pain medications and antibiotics, and check how much blood he had lost.

"Nope, I don't wanna do that Doc," the man told me. "It's not the money. All I want to know is if it's a bullet or a pellet, so I can know which of my neighbors shot him."

I tried my best not to react to his statement, and then I tried my best to change his mind about how to treat his dog, knowing full well that the dog may die in the near future from his injuries. No such luck…he only wanted the x-rays. The x-rays showed the offending object really was a bullet and it has passed directly behind his heart. There had also been a large amount of bleeding into his lungs. The entrance wound was on his left side and the bullet was sitting clear across his thorax on the right side where it landed. This lucky dog missed instant death by inches.

"I'm taking him home," the man told me after confirming that it truly was a bullet. The bullet size made him conclude that it was the Jacksons to the east of his house who shot his dog.

"He'll be fine," he told me.

The man gave me the option of a single medication that I could send home with him. I chose an antibiotic, hoping that the dog wouldn't continue to slowly bleed to death, or get a collapsed lung, or be in severe pain, and that the wound would close on its own. Then, and only then, might my single medication of choice work.

At last, 8:00 a.m. arrived. I sat through an hour of rounds with the specialists who were in no rush at all. They were spry and talkative and spending long periods of time questioning and then educating the interns. I was pretty much fading in my seat and could barely remember the night, never mind clearly round my patients to them. They didn't seem to notice or care.

After we were done, I questioned the surgeons about my Malamute to get their opinion about the likelihood of the dog's survival. I pulled his X-ray up for them to review it.

"You sent that dog home?" was the response I got from one the surgeon after reviewing the x-ray. He had been out of his surgical residency for just about two years.

"Yes," I responded quietly.

I had no energy left to defend myself if they were about to criticize how I treated the dog. The surgeons are used to clients arriving as a referral, at scheduled times, and who are prepared for the expensive surgeries that the pet will need. These guys often have no idea what the clientele are like on an emergency basis.

"They only took x-rays to play CSI investigator?" he asked laughing and then he rolled his eyes. His expression conveyed the same feeling of disbelief and disgust that I had about how the owner chose to care for his pet. I, however, did not have the luxury of rolling my eyes at the owner.

"Yep," I replied, relieved that he seemed to understand.

A year ago this recently graduated surgeon would have been chastising me for not fully treating this dog's injuries. Finally, the sheltered specialists were getting a realistic glimpse and an understanding of what emergency and family veterinarian's lives are like. That one moment, where I could finally see the expression of understanding in his face, was alone worth the agony of the past night.

After rounds and making a few calls, I drove home exhausted. I was having trouble focusing and I struggled to concentrate on the road in front of me. I didn't want to arrive at a destination by ambulance and become my own story at the local human emergency room. I had five hours to get some quality sleep before I needed to return to work. I laid in bed, wide awake. My mind was whirling. I felt beaten up and traumatized. Night of traumas alright, I didn't know who suffered more trauma the previous night – my patients, my clients, my staff, or me. Over and over and over again I thought of the patients that I treated and reviewed the care that I gave them. *Please just let me sleep,* I prayed to the God of Sleep. *Please just let me sleep away the traumas of this night.* I feared these Gods were laughing at me as the events of the night circulated incessantly through my head.

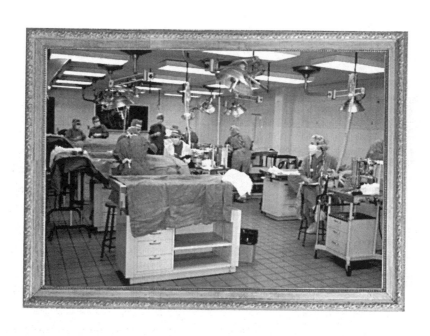

CHAPTER 2

YEAR ONE

"What do I do with the broken toenail which is hanging off this dog's foot at a 90 degree angle?" I called my boss in the middle of the day to ask. Newly out of school and working at my first job as a veterinarian, I was fully prepared to deal with kidney failure, orthopedic diseases, cancer, and uterine infections. But when it came to matters regarding how to treat a broken toenail on a dog, I was clueless.

"Numb it, cut the nail off at the base, and be prepared for a gusher," he told me. He failed to remind me that lidocaine stings terribly and that an 80-pound, hyperactive chocolate lab wasn't going to stand there while I slowly injected the base of his nail with a stinging anesthetic.

"We're just fine," I called to the owner in the next room.

The reality was that my technician and I were being slammed from wall to wall while attempting to hold this exuberant dog down as I stuck a 22-gauge needle into his sensitive toe. Cocoa was not having any part of this. He didn't care that his toenail needed to be cut off or that I was trying to help him. He was not going down easily. After ten minutes of sweet talk, threats and various restraint techniques I succumbed to the conclusion that I just was not getting an anesthetic into that toe. The lidocaine hurts as much as the procedure, I rationalized to myself. Using my nail clippers I snipped the broken nail at its base. Cocoa screamed and jumped from the table. Blood squirted from the nail base and in a matter of minutes covered me, the floor, the wall, and the table in random splatters. As a last attempt to keep him quiet, Karen squatted over him like a cowboy would straddle a bull. This method worked just long enough to allow us to finish our task. As I applied the coagulating stick to the nail end to stop the bleeding, Cocoa yelped again and jerked his foot away, pressing the stick tip against my hand leaving large brown silver nitrate stains on my palms which usually take days to wear off.

"Doing great," I yelled to the owner who was still waiting quietly, perhaps too quietly, in the adjacent room. I hoped she didn't have her ear pressed to the door.

After a few minutes, and with little cooperation from Cocoa, we contained the gusher. We washed the splotches of blood off ourselves, regained our composure, and returned the perturbed dog to its owner.

"How'd that nail go?" yelled my boss from the surgery room the next day.

"Just fine" I said "thanks for your advice."

There was no way I was going to let him in on the details of that fiasco. Many years and seemingly hundreds of broken nails later it feels ludicrous to me that I didn't know what to do with a broken nail when I first started.

I had expected to graduate from veterinary school fully prepared to practice competent and quality medicine when I arrived at my first job. And why wouldn't I? I had just graduated from four grueling years of veterinary school. I was well versed in the husbandry and medicine of an enormous number of species including dogs, cats, cows, horses, swine, llamas, birds, guinea pigs, rats, laboratory monkeys, rabbits, ferrets, hedgehogs, sugar gliders and all of the common zoo animals. I was also an ace when it came to the subjects of meat inspection, diseases of biological warfare, slaughter house diseases, and disease of tropical regions. These courses were included in our program so that veterinarians can act as medical watchdogs and identify diseases that may also affect human health. Apparently the curriculum was designed to educate us about the diseases and medical care of every domesticated animal, farm animal, and zoo animal that has ever been captured worldwide. Even veterinary school administrators have admitted that one of the problems with veterinary school curricula is that there is so much information to absorb that the students are trained "a mile wide and an inch deep." In more recent years, veterinary schools have modified their programs to train students in specialized areas of practice. This curriculum change has helped somewhat to reduce the information overload for new graduates.

Rather than arriving into my new career confident in my abilities as a practitioner, I left veterinary school feeling overwhelmed and unsure of myself. I was brimming with knowledge that was essentially useless in my day-to-day career. Hence, my ignorance in how to treat a broken nail or close a pad laceration or how to open and flush a cat's abscess or how to pull a grass awn from a dog's ear. But no matter, I was a full-fledged expert on the parasitic diseases of captive Zebus in western Africa, a knowledge that would certainly get me far in my career as a small animal veterinarian in the USA.

I landed my first job at a five doctor veterinary practice in a small New England town. The hospital was an old converted dairy barn which was set back from the road and nestled into a corn field. I was thrilled to finally be away from the high pressure, high volume environment of a university veterinary school. I was hired by a husband-and-wife team. By most accounts a husband-wife team is a situation to be avoided at all costs, as the dynamics of a married couple under the same roof are notoriously difficult. As it turns out, both of my employers were kind and fair bosses, each with a fierce sense of humor. As a couple they interacted in a way which translated into a fun-loving work environment. That job lasted for nine-and-a-half wonderful years and started my illustrious career in the most positive and educational manner possible. It was only after I had worked at a series of dysfunctional hospitals that I realized how lucky I was to have had that experience. It can be devastating for a new graduate to start a career in a practice where good quality medicine and good patient care are not practiced. Those first years of your career are your molding years. They set the habits of medicine and surgery that you will continue to practice for many years to come.

At my hospital, I was never left unsupervised and never felt pressured into doing anything that I didn't feel competent or comfortable doing. Unlike medical school, veterinarians are not required to do an internship or residency, and from their first day in practice are legally licensed to do any medical or surgical procedure that they feel cocky enough to tackle. New graduates are sometimes thrown into difficult medical or surgical cases with little or no guidance. Seasoned veterinarians have been known to hire a new graduate and head off immediately for a well needed vacation, leaving the new veterinarian to fend for himself. This usually occurs at the expense of hapless clients and their pets.

One of the first lesson I learned in my early years was how heavily veterinarians depend on their technicians. The best hospitals will hire technicians who are experienced and licensed veterinary technicians. These techs have seen it all and are equally as knowledgeable on how to treat some of the more common medical problems which veterinarians see on a daily basis. That first year my techs patiently showed me how to lance and flush an abscess, administer a vaccine while distracting my patient, restrain a really nasty cat, get a straight X-ray, quiet a beeping fluid pump, and calm an upset client. They took pride in teaching me what they knew about the veterinary field and insuring that I performed up to their hospital standards. I'm sure their pride was fueled by the belief that they had finally found someone who knew less than they did. Rather than be offended by their direction, I found that it was better to take their lessons to heart and relish in the technician's skills and advice. A good technician is essential to the smooth flow of a veterinarian's day and to the proper care of our patients. Behind every good veterinary hospital there is usually a string of conscientious and caring technicians who run the daily show. If you treat them nicely and with the respect that they deserve, your job will go smoothly. Treat them poorly and diminish their skills and accomplishments, and your daily life has just become hell.

"You sure you don't need my help holding?" inquired Belinda, the head technician at my hospital, in regards to my next appointment which was with an injured hamster.

"That's okay. It's just a hamster, I'm sure I am capable of dealing with it." I answered with my most indignant new graduate tone. I sure didn't want my staff thinking I couldn't handle a hamster on my own. A Teddy Bear hamster of all things. It's hard to imagine a cuter, sweeter looking breed than a Teddy Bear. Big eyed, soft fluffy fur, a gentle mouth, and white whiskers that would twitter around its snuffling, pink nose. Thirty grams of rodent cuteness. My patient, named Minnie, belonged to an eight-year-old girl who came in to our hospital with her mother.

"It's Sophie's pet," the mother told me, "Sophie thinks that Minnie has a swollen toe." She was making conspiratorial eye motions at me from across the table. Her gestures were her means of communicating to me to please just humor her daughter's concern.

"I want Sophie to learn what being a responsible pet owner means," she finished. She was stroking her daughter's hair and stopped to gaze fondly down at her while she was speaking.

I reached into the box, where the darling, little ball of fluff was busy rearranging its environment, and I gently enclosed Minnie in my fingers. At that very moment, an intense bolt of pain shot through my finger and reverberated up through the bones of my hand. The pain was so jarring and so intense and so unrelenting that without thought, I reflexively jerked my arm backwards in a single sharp motion. The problem was that the determined Minnie hadn't yet let go. When my hand retracted from the box so did Minnie who still had her sharp, little hamster teeth firmly embedded in my finger.

The owner, her daughter and myself, all watched as Minnie was catapulted from the box while she was still attached to my hand. Minnie's body flew forward and then paused briefly upside down in a perfect little hamster headstand until the centripetal forces forced her to let go of my finger. She then continued solo, accelerating in the shape of an arc, until her body thumped into the wall at a height of about four feet from the floor. The three of us watched in silent horror as Minnie hit the wall backwards and upside down and then almost in cartoon-like fashion slid rhythmically down the wall and landed in a motionless, fuzzy heap on the floor. A morbid, awkward silence filled the room.

I couldn't look at the mother or at the daughter. Sophie started to wail. The mom gave me the nastiest look she could muster. Horrified, I moved over to the puffy fur-ball and lifted Minnie up. Her heartbeat was palpable and, if I looked closely, I could still see the excursions of her little chest wall. She was alive! My emotions were first relief, and then embarrassment that such a thing could have happened. Minnie started to sluggishly move in my hand. I examined her foot before she fully awakened now feeling much more respectful of this little creature. I was just hoping I didn't have to deal with a more serious medical condition now. Minnie continued to show small hamster improvements and I left the room reassured of her recovery when she started actively grooming her fur and gnashing her teeth at me.

I walked into the treatment room clutching my stinging finger. Belinda walked by giving me that "I told you so" look that so many technicians seem to have mastered. It wasn't the first, nor would it be the last time that I was humbled in my career. But I swore that it would be the last time I would ever be humbled by a hamster.

CHAPTER 3

ESCAPES

"**M**ake sure you put Klaus in a cage before you leave the room." I said to the owners of the patient I was treating. Klaus was a 15-year-old red and gold Macaw who had come in for a minor injury to his toe. Macaws are ultra-expensive, exotic birds that are indigenous to South America.

"Don't worry," the owner informed me with overblown confidence, "he never leaves my shoulder. We take him all over the place like this." At that moment, Klaus was sitting contently on his owner's shoulder in the small exam room. He appeared as though he never wanted to abandon his spot. *Uh-huh.* I skeptically thought to myself.

"No really," I cautioned again, "if he gets away in this reception area, or even worse outdoors, we will have one difficult time retrieving him". My boss had recently remodeled our hospital into a modern metropolis. The front entrance and reception room now had a high cathedral ceiling. There was a cat area to the left, a dog area to the right, and a reception desk in the center. Overall the hospital was now a beautiful, spacious, and lofty-ceilinged facility.

As a domesticated bird that rarely flies, Klaus would also be in big trouble if he did decide to fly off while his owner was returning to his car. I could imagine Klaus fluttering away into the nearby pine forest He would spend a few hours, or perhaps a full day, hidden in the branches too frightened to move. With his portly body and lack of stamina he would only be able to fly short distances. If he fell to the ground, he would quickly become a plump, exotic treat to whatever predator was lucky enough to find him.

I left the room reassured by the owner that Klaus would be safely confined to a cage when they left. While the tech was making up Klaus' medications I stepped into the next exam room. A flush-faced and overly pregnant woman was sitting on the bench gently rubbing her round belly. She stood up as I examined her puppy who was there for its third set of vaccines. Staying on schedule with vaccines is crucial in a young dog's life. Few people give that much thought until their lifeless puppy is lying in my hospital, draining fluids from both ends of its body because it contracted a nasty disease like parvovirus.

As I started to vaccinate her puppy, Mrs. Adams suddenly disappeared from my view on the opposite side of the exam table. She was standing there in front of me one minute and then gone the next. I moved around to the other side of the table to find Mrs. Adams lying on her back on the exam room floor with her eyes closed. A stain in her crotch area was seeping down her leg and a pool of urine had formed on the floor.

"Mrs. Adams," I said crouching down next to her. She moaned quietly. I noted the light excursions of her chest, confirmation that she was still breathing. I felt for her pulse which was present and strong.

"Call an ambulance!" I yelled to our technician, Bernice. "Mrs. Adams has fainted. Let them know that she's pregnant." We applied cool washcloths to her face and placed an oxygen mask over her nose. The ambulance arrived a short time later. The EMTs placed Mrs. Adams on a gurney and began wheeling her out of the exam room.

As I held the door open for them, I noticed that the door to the adjacent room was opening. Klaus' owners, tired of waiting for my return, had heard the ensuing commotion and ventured out into the reception room. Klaus was still perched on his owner's shoulder. Despite my repeated warnings, they were still convinced that their trusted bird would never leave. Klaus, on the other hand, had different ideas. He took one look at the covered mound being wheeled away on the gurney to his right, squawked an ear-piercing scream, and flew off into the rafters. Startled by the noise, the EMTs looked up but continued to wheel Mrs. Adams through the reception area as if nothing unusual were happening.

Klaus seized this opportunity to fly in large circles around the room, making loud whirring noises as he ungracefully flapped his wings, sending showers of red feathers onto the recumbent woman. Squawking at the top of his lungs, as only a Macaw can do, Klaus' screams reverberated around the hollow room. He made several kamikaze-like sweeps at the moving gurney and then gleefully made more laps around the room. The not-so-easily rattled EMTs ignored Klaus' antics and vocalizations and continued their path to the front door. Their imperturbable composure gave the pretense that screaming, swooping Macaws are a normal part of their job description. But when they shut the front glass door I could see the look of relief on their faces followed by large grins which belied the stony calmness that they had been emanating inside of the hospital. They were happy to be leaving the chaos behind them. I completely understood. I wished that I could do the same. "Welcome to the circus that is my life," is what I wanted to say to them and enjoy the rest of the day which actually seems to me to be a very peaceful job compared to what I have to deal with each day.

A patient's escape from a veterinary hospital is a rare event but when it does happen, it becomes every hospital and insurance company's nightmare. Animals most commonly escape when they are taken out for walks or when they dash outside through an open door. Hospitals try to take precautions such as double leashing dogs, walking them in specific confined areas, or placing identification neckbands on them when they are hospitalized, but the possibility of an escape always exists.

When an animal does escape it is a frightening event for everyone involved. At one hospital where I worked many years later, a dog managed to escape our facility when it slipped its collar as it was being taken outside for a walk. Seeing a big opportunity to flee its captors, the dog ran off into the dark night. The technicians and the doctor, my friend

Robin, spent hours searching for her but with no luck. Robin was unable to reach the owners by phone. Frantic with worry she called me. The panic was obvious in her voice: "I just keep praying that she won't be killed. And that she will go to a safe spot where we can find her."

Adding to our concerns was the presence of an extremely busy four lane road just one block from the hospital.

The following morning Robin called me back. This time she sounded ecstatic. "We found her," she said. "She was sitting on the steps at the front door of the church down the street. The minister found her when he arrived. God answered my prayers. He brought her back to the safest spot he could think of." I nodded my head, happy to agree with her argument for divine intervention.

In a bizarre reversal of circumstances from the norm of the veterinary world, I once found myself breaking back into my hospital with one of our patients. I was doing my Sunday morning examinations. In the hopes of being able to get in some skiing that day, I had arrived at the hospital particularly early. I took a fat beagle named Jenny out for a walk. Jenny was hospitalized for progressive kidney disease. I was trying to maneuver Jenny, her leash, and her IV bag in my arms as we walked outside. As soon as I stepped onto the sidewalk, I heard the sound of the newly installed latch closing behind me. It was five o'clock on a wintery New England morning and I was locked outside with a sick dog, her IV fluid bag, and fluid line. My jacket and keys were inside and the nearest neighbors were a quarter of a mile away. I had visions of walking down the street and knocking on the neighbor's door, with my patient and all of her medical paraphernalia to ask them if I could use their phone. It all seemed a bit too absurd and I decided against that plan to avoid giving them an unwelcome Sunday morning fright.

After some concentrated thinking I came up with an alternative plan. My clever idea was to try and break back into the hospital by accessing the outside dog pens. I remembered that if I climbed over the outer chain link fence and then into the exterior dog pens, I may be able to force open the hatchet type door that separates the kennels from the pens and then crawl back into the indoor boarder's cages. Since I was terrified of leaving Jenny outside alone where she could potentially escape, I decided she would have to join me in my caper of burglarizing the hospital.

"I wish you weren't so fat," I muttered to Jenny as I lifted her and pushed her rotund body and IV bag over the fence. Jenny seemed a bit aghast at the indignity of being shoved over a chain link fence on a cold, dark morning when she should have been inside sleeping.

Stage one…complete. I prayed that no passersby would notice us.

Stage two involved climbing over the second fence that comprised the chain linked wall of the outdoor dog pens. The dogs in the kennels were barking loudly in protest of our intrusion but that did not deter us.

Stage three was by far the trickiest part of the plan. It involved Jenny and me wheedling ourselves through the small hatchet door that separated the outdoor pens from the indoor cages. I wedged the hatchet door upwards and then slowly pushed rotund Jenny through the tiny opening into the cage inside. Inch by inch, in a linear worming fashion, I followed Jenny by squeezing myself through the door which was designed for small dogs. "Don't bite me Jenny," I thought as my face and then my body came directly at her within the tight confines of the inner cage. Getting pushed into close confinement with an animal you do not know, even if it is your partner in crime at that moment, is never a smart idea. Now Jenny and I were enclosed together in the cage that was barely large enough to fit only one of us. God forbid the morning employees should arrive now to find us guiltily smushed into a cage side-by-side staring out at them like confined circus animals. I reached outside the cage, unlatched the door, and gratefully stepped into the warmth of the hospital.

Mission complete.

"Don't you dare tell anyone," I whispered to Jenny as I returned the relieved, and somewhat disgusted-looking dog to her cage. She needed no encouragement to scamper in and away from the weirdo who had taken her for a walk on this particular morning.

CHAPTER 4

A PEOPLE BUSINESS

The veterinary business is not an animal business, it is a people business. Aspiring veterinarians who are entering the profession because they don't enjoy dealing with people have a large reality check coming to them because at the end of every leash, and holding every cat carrier is an owner. An owner who considers his pet a family member, and who arrives at our hospital worried, sad, protective, or terrified for it. And as a veterinarian you must always keep in mind the extremely important fact that it is the owner not the patient who pays the bills.

Strong emotions are often evoked in people who unexpectedly find themselves within the walls of a veterinary hospital. These emotions may be centered on losses, either animal or human, that the owner has previously experienced. Arriving with a sick pet cradled in their arms, owners will spill stories to me that I am sure they would never choose to share with a complete stranger in any other circumstance. Despite our constant immersion in other people's grief and pain the skill of how to counsel a bereaved person or how to deal with our own emotions which are triggered by their stories is not a subject which we were ever formally taught in school. Most veterinarians learn this important skill the hard way by becoming immersed in other people's grief over and over and over again in the course of their daily jobs.

During one busy shift, a German shepherd was brought back to my treatment area to be examined. The dog's neck was covered with blood and there was a red stained bandage wrapped loosely around his head. The source of the bleeding was from somewhere beneath the bandage. As I unwrapped the bloody cloth, I discovered that the upper third of Charlie's right ear was missing. Instead of the upright and conical shape that a Shepherd's ear should have, the ear was now tattered and bloody, and the center was torn out. The ear was in the shape of a large 'V,' and was hanging down from his head at an odd angle.

"My female dog attacked him for no reason at all," the distraught looking owner explained to me in the exam room. "They started fighting in the living room, it continued down the hall, and then they tumbled into my bedroom. She was gripping his head in her mouth. I could not get her off of him. She wouldn't let go." He was twisting the tissues that he was holding in his hands as he continued speaking to me, "They've lived together for two years now and occasionally they get into scraps but nothing like this.'

The whole fight and the events that followed had obviously unnerved this burly young man who had pirate loop earrings in each ear and a tattoo on his neck. Unexpectedly the man started to shake and tears started to stream down his face. I hate to see men cry and I think men hate to have me see them cry. I especially dislike seeing tough-looking men cry since they work very hard on maintaining their image. I made myself busy at the sink in order to give Charlie's owner a moment to compose himself. He was obviously unnerved by the evening's events. It is scary to have the pets in your family viciously attacking each other within the walls of your own home.

The injuries didn't look particularly serious, there were a few minor punctures on the dog's body that would readily heal, and a scrape across his nose which had no future consequence. The ear laceration seemed to be the worst of Charlie's injuries, but once that wound healed he would continue to go about his happy dog life without a second thought about his tattered looking ear. But I understood that the harmony in this man's home and the trust that he had in his pets could not be so easily repaired. Still, his reaction to his dogs' fighting seemed extreme considering the fairly minor nature of the injuries. I tried to be nonchalant and convey through my body language that crying is a common occurrence within the walls of a veterinary hospital.

"Don't worry, Charlie is okay. We can repair his ear without problems. We'll have him looking as handsome as ever in a jiffy," I told him keeping my voice light and my tone reassuring.

"It's not that. Charlie is my brother's dog. I was taking care of Charlie until my brother returned." The words faded out followed by a long awkward pause as he tried to compose himself. "The only thing is that my brother never returned home. He was killed in Iraq six months ago and I am not taking very good care of his dog."

He bent over and started violently sobbing again. It was then that I understood that his tears had nothing to do with his dog's ear or his dogs' fighting. This was about the extreme sadness and pain in his own life, a pain which was now manifesting itself through the violent scuffle his dogs had just had. It was also about the lack of control that we have when it comes to events in our lives. I fully understand lack of control over the circumstances in our lives. In fact, I am an unintentional expert. I knew that the only thing I could offer to him at that moment in time, was to sit with him. I am the purest form of an empathetic ear.

As I repaired Charlie's ear I contemplated the circumstances that seem to so frequently engulf me into the traumas of my clients' lives. I bet the local mechanic does not get burly men crying in his shop and telling him about the death of his brother after their transmission blows. I'm sure the dentist doesn't hear about his clients divorce and the nasty custody battles over their children and family pets. But the mere act of experiencing a medical problem with your pet seems to open the gates of sorrow in an individual at the veterinarian's office.

Each animal and each owner that comes into my hospital has his own history. And it is a history that I am sure to hear about if I spend enough time with them. These revelations from people disturb me as I am so easily sucked into the sadness of their personal lives. Charlie's story left a sense of gloom over me which I carried around with me the whole day.

33

Several weeks later an elderly woman arrived at my emergency room. She was escorted by a younger woman who turned out to be her kind neighbor. It was apparent that the elderly woman was suffering from a neurologic problem, perhaps Parkinson's disease. The woman was able to communicate effectively enough but she was having trouble controlling her body motions. In addition to the characteristic persistent tremors that Parkinson's patients get, her upper body rolled repeatedly in large waves as she was speaking to me. I tried hard to focus on her words and not be distracted by her rhythmic rolling. Her dog, YoYo, a pleasantly plump Cocker Spaniel, vivaciously wagged her stub of a tail each time that I put my hands on her. YoYo had not been eating well the last few days and now had developed a bad case of runny diarrhea. This poor, frail woman was not only trying to care for herself, but now was trying to manage a dog that was dripping diarrhea throughout her house.

"Let's keep YoYo in the hospital until she's better," I suggested "and then you won't have to deal with cleaning up this mess."

"This would all be so much easier if my husband hadn't just died," she said matter-of-factly. I looked at her more closely, recalculating the stresses that were going on in her life.

"He died two weeks ago. Died suddenly in his sleep from bleeding into his brain." Not one single tear emerged. Not an ounce of emotion was expressed on her face. "I wish his children would just leave me alone." She finished the sentence in a higher pitched voice. "They want his things and now his money. They are trying to rob me."

Her face remained blank but her undulations increased in frequency. I nodded my head sympathetically, yet not sure of how to respond to this disturbing news.

"They never called or visited him when he was alive. They haven't seen him in two years. Now, suddenly they want his things. They're trying to rob me of everything that we shared together. YoYo is the only thing of his that they don't want."

Particularly with a bad case of runny diarrhea, is the monologue that I finish for her in my head.

Here we go again. One moment I'm a veterinarian simply trying to treat a dog's diarrhea and the next minute, without any provocation, I become their confidante and am emerged in the torrid details of my client's life. *Once again a dogs poop has transgressed into the scoop on my client's life poop,* is the less than humorous thought that ran through my head. It's a position that if given a choice I would prefer not to be immersed in. No pun intended. And then because I couldn't help it, sympathy, empathy and outrage welled up inside of me as she continued to speak. *Careful,* I remind myself, *you don't know all sides of this story.*

I remembered my Grandma Sally's past warnings "There are always three sides to a story, yours, mine and the truth." I bit my tongue sharply as a physical remembrance to keep my opinions to myself and mentally thanked grandma for her everlasting wisdom.

I brought YoYo back to the prep room. I now knew why YoYo had a bad case of diarrhea. I knew without having to run a single test. YoYo's stool was runny because she was living in a sad and stressful environment. "A proper history will give you fifty percent of your answers as to what is wrong with an animal," I often find myself saying to the newly arriving interns at our hospital. Most of them are eager to run the most sophisticated diagnostic tests to get their answers when often a large clue to what is wrong with the animal is directly in front of them. I found myself cooing to YoYo, and lining her cage with the softest and most colorful blankets that we had. When I had the spare time I would sit with YoYo and pet her and reassure her that she was in a safe and friendly place. Later that night I transferred her care over to Robin, the veterinarian who was working the overnight shift. She would be the veterinarian who would discharge YoYo to her owner the next day.

"Her owner is an elderly woman with Parkinson's. Her husband just died and her family isn't supportive." I explained to her. "I am keeping YoYo here, partly to treat her diarrhea but mostly because her owner needs the break." Robin nodded her head in an understanding manner. She also understood perfectly. Robin is one of the kindest, most compassionate people that I know and that is part of what makes her such a good vet. She too understood that she needed to care for YoYo with the knowledge and empathy that her carefree dog life had been dramatically and adversely affected by the death of her owner.

Perhaps that is the lesson here. Perhaps that is why people share these stories with us. They want our medical care to go beyond the clinical therapy alone. They want us to understand the history and the emotions which have created or exacerbated their animal's disease. If we have that knowledge, then we can encompass that extra bit of compassion and tenderness into their medical care at a time when the animal may need just a bit more. Having this knowledge would also mean that we can care for the owners with just a little more compassion then we would have had we not had that knowledge. Tomorrow when she released YoYo to her owner, Robin would speak to the woman with clarity and with compassion and with a hopeful and positive tone. Robin would know to communicate through her body language and through her choice of words how she understood that this was a very fragile and frightening time for both of them.

CHAPTER 5

BITE ME

When I tell people that I am a veterinarian there are usually a few predictable responses that follow. A favorite response is: "I have a niece...or a grandson... or a daughter... who wants to be a veterinarian." I want to tell them to get in line because becoming a veterinarian seems to be the aspiration of many a child, right behind becoming a fireman, a policeman, or an astronaut. It is not an easy pursuit and not for the faint of heart. Their relative will need to have resilience, good grades, perseverance and the stomach to be a veterinarian. I applaud each of these people's dreams and I sincerely wish them the best. Even after all of this time I still believe veterinary medicine is an incredibly rewarding career.

"I used to have a dog who ..." is another popular response to the revelation of my profession. And then I hear stories of how Fluffy liked to steal the newspaper, or how Muffy used to herd the children around, or how Cocoa could jump any fence they had ever built. Although I have heard similar stories over and over again, I still listen because I know that Fluffy's story is unique and important to the person telling the story.

Sooner or later someone asks one of the more provocative questions: "Have you ever been bitten?"

"Well, yes of course," I respond "we all have."

Being bitten is an unfortunate occupational hazard in veterinary medicine. One of the few career fields in the world where you have to worry, literally rather than metaphorically, about the sharp teeth of your customers. We all get better and better at avoiding being bitten but, if you're in this field long enough, eventually it will happen.

The last time a survey was taken by the Center for Disease Control was in 2003. The survey revealed that 4.7 million people were bitten by a dog and over 800,000 people were treated at a hospital for bite injuries. In 2013, 32 people died from dog bite related injuries. The majority of those bites involved children between the ages of five and nine. Statistically, you are more likely to be bitten by your own dog or a friend's dog than by a stranger's dog. Children are more likely to be bitten than adults because they are at eye level with the dog. They are also more physical with the pup and may inadvertently fall over it or naively taunt it. Children tend to be loud and squeal and run away which can instigate a dog to chase, grab or bite the child. A dog who is fearful, dominant, or in pain may perceive these childhood behaviors as threatening. Any breed can be implicated in a dog bite, but in one study German Shepherds, Labradors, Chihuahuas, and Rottweilers were listed amongst the most likely to bite. Different studies have implicated different breeds as the most likely to bit. There results may be more representative of the number of people owning these popular breeds than their actual likelihood to bite as a breed.

Over the course of my career I've seen many injuries occur in a veterinary environment. I've seen animals bite people out of pain, fear, territorial instinct, maternal protection, or while taking their last gasping breath in an attempt to live. I've seen a cat leap out of its cage and wrap its legs like an octopus around a veterinarian's head gnawing away at his face the whole time. One technician had her arm broken in two by the mouth of a Chow that she was trying to coax out of its cage. Removing an animal from the confinement of a cage can be one of the most vulnerable positions for a person to be. I watched another technician get thrown into a wall after a large Mastiff she was holding threw its head back, hitting her so hard in the chin that her jaw was broken. Cat bites can create some really nasty wounds. The bacteria from a cat bite can potentially result in successive surgeries or weeks or months of wound care to correct the damage that might occur. Some bites may even lead to permanent mobility disorders. Although cat bites are nasty what is more intimidating is the potential of being bitten by an animal whose bite may be fatal to you. I remember clearly how frightening it was for me to euthanize a raccoon who was considered highly likely to be infected with rabies. It was ominously clear that I could not make any mistakes with my sedation techniques.

When working in the exam room, if the patient is trying to bite me I take it away from its owner. This serves a few purposes. Firstly, dogs who are trying to bite me with their owner present may stop trying to bite me when their owners are away. Secondly, I am worried about the owner's safety. Dogs who are frightened or in pain may not hesitate to bite at the person nearest to them, which is often their owner. And on a legal basis we don't want that to happen within the walls of our hospital, since we may be legally responsible if a pet bites his owner while on our premises.

Veterinarians in farm medicine are more likely to sustain fatal injuries than small animal practitioners. One veterinarian told me how he was knocked over by a llama which then proceeded to stand over his fallen body and paw at him fiercely.

"I thought I was going to die. Thankfully the owner came out, saw what was happening and shooed him away. I was sure I was a goner," recounted the large and muscular man as we sat on our lunch break sipping coffee.

This burly veterinarian wasn't someone I could imagine being intimidated by a llama. I suddenly developed a new respect for the power of llamas. I was well aware of the dangers from a well-placed kick by a horse or an out-of-control cow but I had never considered llamas to be dangerous animals. I heard about one colleague who died trying to haul a cow out of a pond where it had become bogged down. Somehow the young vet got entwined in the mud and line along with the struggling cow and never emerged from the murky water. It is an odd and quirky death for a person who is in an odd and quirky profession. I remember a zoo veterinarian lamenting that poisonous snakes always seem to have medical problems in their mouths. The implication of a bite from one of those creatures is clear. The risks of our profession are multiple and haphazard.

Most dogs don't scare me but I've been badly frightened by a few. Dogs in packs particularly frighten me. I can remember being outside the limits of a small village in Thailand. My friend and I had gone to bathe in the river. On our way back to the village we were surrounded by a pack of scrawny, mangy, wild-appearing dogs. They circled us slowly moving as a group, one would dart in and nip at our heels and then run back to the pack while a second and then third dog would approach us, all crouching down as they moved towards us. Dogs in third world countries are scary. These dogs are often unsocialized, usually hungry, and are fearful from having rocks tossed at them. Most frightening of all is the fact that in these countries there is a good chance that they may be carriers of rabies. Packs of dogs are quite a different entity from dogs as individuals. In a group their confidence feeds off of each other. They work together as a pack to confine and kill their prey. An animal of prey is exactly what I felt like as we headed back to the village, stalked and surrounded by this unfriendly, feral group of dogs. My friend Liz was panicking.

"Don't run," I kept hissing softly under my breath. "Don't run. They'll kill you if you run."

She restrained herself from this understandable instinct, but I could tell from the panicked look on her face that it wasn't easy for her. We walked slowly and silently, side-stepping our way back to the village. Inch by inch we gained ground until we made it through the village gates. That was an experience I won't easily forget. Nor will I forget how easily animals can intimidate you when they act together as a pack. At home, in a local newspaper, I read how an elderly man was killed by a pack of semi-wild farm dogs when he entered the farm to speak to the owner. *How horrific*, I thought, but then remembering my experience in Thailand it didn't surprise me. Elderly people are frail and unsteady and are easy targets for a pack of unsocialized farm dogs.

On occasion I'm scared by dogs in the exam room. It's not the snapping dogs that cower in the corner that bother me. I know what to expect from these dogs. It's the dogs that look me in the face, with dilated pupils, and walk towards me growling. These dogs frighten me because they are bold, aggressive and not intimidated even outside of their home environment. Usually I can read the body posture of an animal to know if I need to be cautious. If I am concerned or if I know that in the course of my exam I may hit a tender spot, I will suggest to the owner that we muzzle their pup which prevents any future problems.

"Just keeping him honest," I say to the owner as I gently slip on a muzzle.

On occasion I misread a dog. My first impression from its body language is that it is friendly. And then as I lean over and start to look into its eyes or examine its teeth, when suddenly its upper lip raises and I am faced with a set of teeth inches from my face. This is a very scary and vulnerable position to be in. All I can do is freeze and back off slowly hoping to not antagonize the dog into further aggressive action.

"Don't worry he would never bite," owners will tell me with confidence as Fluffy "smiles" at me with his teeth bared. *Great then you go and put your face near a stranger's snarling dog and see if you would trust that person's assessment of whether or not their dog will not bite you,* is the response that circles through my mind.

Sometimes it is not until after the animal has snapped at me that the owner will decide to mention that the dog has a history of biting. Since owners never want to believe that their dog could hurt someone, they are reluctant to have a muzzle placed on their pet. This is one of the few things that really upsets me. *Why would you not mention that to me before I approached your dog? Would it have been better to have seen my face bloody and mangled by his fangs than to have mentioned that sweet Snoopy has the potential to bite?* Seemingly, some people would rather see us injured than admit that their dog may need a muzzle.

Another oddly absurd comment which I hear fairly frequently is: "Don't worry he'll clamp down but he won't break your skin." They say this with full sincerity, never doubting that it could result in a different outcome.

Really? We're talking about millimeters of difference in a dog who's doesn't like or trust the stranger in the white coat in front of him. See that snarling hundred pound Rottweiler over there? I've heard from his owners that he's really quite sweet and the growling is all talk. He never breaks the skin when he grabs your arm. Go over there and touch his laceration on his leg.

When I was younger and less experienced I used to give in to an owner's wishes to not muzzle their pets. I was afraid of upsetting them. Not anymore. Sorry, it's my hands, my face and my career. *I am sorry if you are offended but here's a muzzle for your dog who I do not entirely trust. Please put it on.*

Over the years I've had numerous minor cuts and scratches, but as of yet I've only been seriously injured twice in my career. The first time was in my first year out of veterinary school. I went into the exam room to remove the sutures from the side of the face of a German Shepherd where a laceration had been repaired two weeks earlier. The shepherd was eying me uneasily at the end of his leash so I put a muzzle on him. I removed most of the sutures working around the muzzle and then took it off thinking that I was finished. After the muzzle was off, the owners noticed that one suture was left. The dog had remained quiet through the suture removal so I made the bad decision of not replacing the muzzle to remove the last stitch. I started feeling around the side of his face when without warning the dog lunged up, knocking me to the floor. I found myself on my back with a large growling German Shepherd hovering over me. His snarling face was three inches from my own. Blood was staining my shirt where he had taken his first bite in my armpit region. His lips were raised and a low rumble was emerging from his throat. I could feel his breath on my face. I knew that with a single lunge at my throat he could tear a major artery. The stunned owners were standing in the corner not moving.

"Grab his leash," I whispered afraid to raise my voice with the dogs face so close to mine. Regaining their composure the owners pulled their dog off of me and held him close to them, patting him. I stood up and shakily wiped myself off. The owners looked about as terrified and shaken up as I did.

"Everything okay?" asked my technician Karen, popping her head into the room.

No, everything was not okay. I was shaking, frightened and acutely aware once again of how rapidly life can change. I could have been killed because of a single suture that would have fallen out on its own in a week. With tears welling in my eyes, I walked out of the room to compose myself. I was wearing a dressy white shirt that day. That morning I had put it on thinking that wearing a white shirt to work was a mistake as the odds were it would soon be covered in yellow or brown stains. Now, instead, a large red stain was seeping along the shirts fabric with several tooth punctures near the center. I hung the red-stained shirt in my closet that evening as a forever reminder of the hazards of my job. The blood stained blouse in my closet would be a way of immortalizing the violence that had affected my life on that day.

Sometimes we need aggressive methods to restrain overly aggressive dogs. These methods are necessary if we are faced with a dangerous dog. A "rabies pole" is a long rigid pole that has a retractable noose on one end. It is commonly used by animal control officers. Most veterinary hospitals own one as well. The device allows a person to stand at a distance from a dangerous dog and tighten the noose from the far end of the pole. The pole keeps the dog at a distance and prevents him from being able to contact the handler of the pole. If a rabies pole is not available an alternate method is to slip a lead around the dog's neck and pull the leash around a pole or stanchion until the dog's head is stabilized against the pole. This creates a choking hold at the front end which then allows a second person to safely give the dog a sedative injection in its rump. Another primitive yet effective restraint method is to close a door around a dogs shoulders as we walk it through a doorway. This method pins the aggressive dog in the door frame with its biting end on one side of the door and the back end on the other side which allows a person at the back end to safely give an injection. These last two methods are reserved for dogs that are so aggressive that no one, including its owner, can get close enough to muzzle it or give it a sedation injection without fear of being mauled.

The second time that I was badly bitten occurred many years after the first event. I have had a few minor scrapes and a few close calls during the intervening years but nothing particularly memorable until the day a young Chihuahua puppy came into my emergency room. It was 8:05 in the evening, five minutes after my shift had ended. The puppy was snapping and snarling and lashing out at anyone who went near it. The techs were surrounding the dog and trying to contain it. Small dogs are easily intimidated if they are overly crowded. Plus this was a six-month-old puppy. If puppies are showing signs of aggression it is generally because they're spoiled and no one has ever used the word, "no" with them. I went over to help. I asked the technician to pass the puppy who was wrapped in a towel over to me, hind end first. Just like you always pass a knife to a person handle first, you always pass a small dog or cat to a person bite-free end first.

"Be careful Doc, he's an angry one," said Sean, reluctantly passing him over.

I believed that if I could hold the pup in my hands then I would be able to calm him down enough to get a muzzle on him. That was a serious misjudgment on my part. I did not recognize quickly enough that this puppy was not just a naughty puppy, he was a neurologically abnormal puppy. The puppy had become violently aggressive at home due to a medical condition which was starting to affect his brain. He was ravenously biting everybody in his home, when earlier in the day he had been a sweet and loving puppy. There are several medical explanations as to why this puppy's behavior was so rapidly changing. Trauma or a sudden increase in pressure within the skull are a few of the potential causes that a veterinarian would consider if we were trying to find an answer to why his behavior had changed so rapidly.

I held the puppy in the towel with the biting end faced away from me. I talked to him in a soft cooing voice trying to calm him down. When he seemed quiet I removed the towel covering his eyes. It was only then that I understood that this was not just a temperamental puppy. Most dogs are biting to try and get away from you. This puppy was biting to get at me. In slow motion the puppy seemed to stretch up and grow tall. Like a cobra striking, he first leaned backwards and then with sharp intention struck out and up at my face. In one precise motion he latched onto my lower lip and tore down sharply with his two upper canine teeth. The puppy's well placed bite cut two distinct slices on my lower lip so that my lip was now effectively sliced free of my mouth and hanging down off my gums.

In shock I put the pup down. The injury hurt, but not as bad as I would have expected. There was a shocked silence in the room as the other employees looked at me. The pervasive silence informed me that some significant damage had been done. I felt at my face to assess the damage. My fingers came back covered with blood. I was afraid to look in the mirror. I didn't want to know how badly I had been disfigured. At that moment, ignorance truly was bliss.

After applying pressure to my mouth with a gauze, I mentally prepared myself, and walked into the bathroom. My image in the mirror shocked me. I looked like the Joker from the Batman movies. Two vertical red lines extended down to my chin creating a bizarre grin-like expression. Applying pressure, I replaced my lower lip and pushed it back where it belonged. Only then did the reflection look like my own.

"I'd better get to a doctor," I told my overly silent team of technicians.

I drove myself to the nearest emergency hospital where they immediately ushered me into a room. I'm sure that it is bad for business to leave a disfigured woman sitting in the waiting room.

I started to worry about the other realities of this bite. When a dog becomes suddenly aggressive, rabies has to be on the list of possible causes. I had worked in a high prevalence rabies state in the past so I was used to some of the worries and precautions of working with potentially rabid animals. We used to euthanize rabid raccoons regularly at the veterinary hospital where I worked in New England. If you were accidentally bitten by one of those rabid animals you may very well die as a result of it. This state had a very low rate of rabies in domestic and wild animals so the likelihood that this puppy was rabid was pretty low. Still, I had just been bitten in the face by a neurologically abnormal dog and that made it scary. The rabies virus travels along nerves and if you're bitten in the face it will travel up the nerves called the cranial nerves which have a very short and direct connection to the brain. This means that the incubation period to develop rabies if you are bitten in the face is much shorter than if you're bitten in the hand.

I had been vaccinated against rabies when I was in vet school but that was a long time ago and I had not had my titers checked recently to see if I was still adequately protected. I mentioned to the attending ER doctor my concern about rabies. To my astonishment he answered: "Let's just wait and see."

I wanted to say: *If I wait to see if I show any clinical signs, I'll be a dead woman you dumbass!* But I refrained, as he was in the middle of sewing up my face. Not the time to make him angry. Rabies needs to be prevented not treated. Once you start to show signs of the disease there is a good chance that you have reached the end of your line.

Luckily the people at the animal state health lab felt a little differently about the situation. They recognized the life threatening consequences of a bite to the face by an abnormally behaving dog. They even elected to send a lab technician in on a national holiday just to run the test. Running a rabies test means that the animal in question needs to be euthanized and the brain sent to the lab for submission. There is no other reliable or more pleasant way of testing an animal for rabies. Since the puppy was not responding to treatment and the family could not manage a crazed and out-of-control puppy they agreed to put the unhealthy pup down. Thankfully for everyone involved, the test was negative.

I went back to work with the Joker smile now sutured onto my face. The fresh sutures were an unsightly reminder, once again, of how risky my profession can be. No one expects to come to work fresh faced and smiling and leave that evening disfigured. But that risk is real. It is lurking in the daily routine of every veterinary hospital and is a possibility with every animal with which we interact. In the midst of the mundane interactions of a regular business day it can be a risk which is easy to lose sight of which is why basic safety precautions and mindful handling of every animal is so important in this profession.

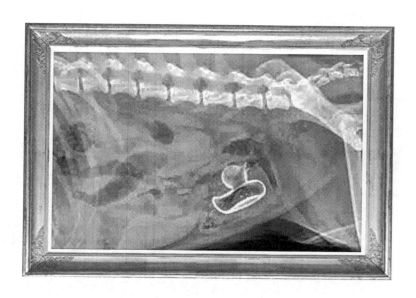

CHAPTER 6

EAT IT

Dogs will eat the oddest things. Labradors, beagles and golden retrievers come to mind first as breeds that have a reputation for eating anything which fits into their mouths. But most certainly we cannot discriminate this as a specific trait of a dog's breed or lineage. Any dog from the filthiest mutt to the most well-coiffed show dog is susceptible to eating an inappropriate object if given the chance. Our canine friends are lucky in the sense that the majority of objects that they apprehend will pass through them unscathed. But this means that the dog who chooses an object which is too large, or too sharp, or too awkwardly shaped to slither its way through eighteen feet of intestines, will end up at a veterinary hospital needing major surgery to remove the object from the spot in his intestinal tract where it has become lodged. This is a painful experience on a number of levels. It is painful for the unfortunate animal who has the object stuck in its intestines, and it can be an equally painful experience for the owner who is forced to seek veterinary care for his delinquent pet.

In veterinary school, a young lab was admitted to our surgery service. We suspected that he had an object stuck in his intestines. Upon entering the hospital the dog was admitted at the front desk. He was then placed in an exam room where his history was taken by a technician. The attending veterinary student looked at him first and then the schools clinician examined him. Blood was drawn by a lab technician and two radiology technicians took his x-rays. The radiologist read out the results of the x-rays. Later that evening the surgeon and a surgical intern performed a surgery on the dog and removed a lodged contraceptive diaphragm from the pup's intestinal tract. As I was the veterinary student on the surgery rotation who had admitted the dog, I was given the duty of letting the owner know what her dog had eaten.

"Your dog is recovering nicely, Ms. Emmett. He had an intestinal obstruction." I prayed that she would be happy with that answer but she inevitably asked the question that everyone wants to know when they've just spent several thousand dollars to save their dog's life.

"What was it?"

"It was a diaphragm," I answered in the most nonchalant and neutrally professional voice that I was capable of speaking.

"Oh great," she said covering her eyes with her hand," I was wondering where that went. It's bad enough that I have to be here, watching my pet in all of this pain, spending all of this money, and be without my birth control, but now I have to walk around with the entire university hospital knowing the details of my sex life." I didn't try to convince her otherwise.

Dogs seem to have an inherent ability to embarrass their owners. I remember one of my clients describing how her dogs had dragged the contents of her bathroom garbage can, which included several sanitary pads and an old bra, through the living room as she was entertaining her husband's important business associates. Another recalled how she cooked a lovely steak meal for friends. While they sat in the living room socializing the two dogs covertly ate the entire steak. The guests ended up gnawing on frozen pizza while the dogs snored contentedly with bloated bellies.

The variety of objects that we remove surgically seems endless. I have seen knives, jewelry, cell phones, toys and stuffed animals removed from the intestinal tract of dogs. I have also seen tennis balls, shoes, diamond rings, fake teeth, shish kebab skewers, and Barbie doll parts removed. Socks and underwear seem to be favorite delicacies of canine connoisseurs nationwide. I am sure that in the course of my career to this point I have seen more lady's panties removed from a dog's intestines then are laid out at the local Victoria's Secrets front table on any particular day. There does not seem to be a preference for thong, brief, high cut, cotton, polyester or silk. It seems that any style of panty will suffice for indiscriminating canines.

Most objects that are eaten will either pass through or become stuck within a week's time. Some objects stick around a little longer. One journal article described a rubber ducky that was removed from an eight-year-old dog's abdomen. The x-ray showed a perfect little plastic ducky sitting in the middle of his stomach. The ducky was in there for so long that it had become wooden in consistency, making it highly visible on x-rays when they were finally taken. The owners insisted that their dog had not had access to a ducky for over six years and that its rubber ducky had one day mysteriously disappeared… a six-year mystery which was now solved. At the residence of my first veterinary job in New England, I passed by the surgery suite just in time to see my boss pulling a long stretch of a cassette tape out of a dog's intestine.

"What in the world would entice him to eat this?" he muttered. He then rationalized a plausible explanation to himself which did not necessitate my reply. "It must be country music. Nothing else could possibly be worth the agony of all of this," he mumbled continuing to pull loops and loops of tape from the dog's inflamed intestines.

Any intestinal foreign body has the potential to be dangerous. It is most likely to be life threatening if the object becomes stuck and tears a hole in the wall of the intestine. Severe vomiting, inappetence, and pain are all warning signs of an intestinal obstruction. These are usually progressive signs which worsen over the course of a few days, but sometimes the things that they eat become life threatening in a more immediate fashion.

One morning a mom and her teenage son arrived at our clinic with their young Standard Poodle. "Something is wrong," they told me worriedly, "she's just not acting normal."

Veterinarians universally refer to this vague type of history as an 'ADR', which is a humorous veterinary slang for just Ain't Doin' Right, doc. In this profession unless we take the time to ask specific questions we will frequently get that kind of history. The mother explains that Chelsea had been outside playing when she stopped suddenly and refused to move.

On first glance, Chelsea looked normal. She walked into our hospital willingly and even offered an unenthusiastic wag of her tail when I spoke to her. There was nothing on my initial survey to indicate a serious problem. Yet, she just wasn't the bouncing playful Standard Poodle I expected. I asked the owner a few key questions: "Any possible exposure to toxins? Is it a fenced back yard or does she run loose? Were there any other unusual behaviors recently?" Next, following a set sequence that I use with every animal, I began my physical exam of Chelsea. I looked at her eyes, then checked her ear canals, checked out her gums and teeth, and felt the lymph nodes beneath her jaw. I then gently opened her mouth to look inside. There was a moderate amount of mucous and foam in the back of her throat but nothing else of significance. As I started to close her mouth I caught a quick glimpse of blue near the back of her throat. Wiping away the foam, which was obscuring my view, I could better visualize the object which turned out to be a blue convex rubber sphere. My mood changed rapidly.

"Your dog has a ball caught in the back of her throat," I explained. "If the ball moves backwards at all this could quickly become a critical situation because it will obstruct her larynx and she will not be able to breathe. If it is tightly lodged and I am unable to remove it quickly enough, I may have to perform an emergency tracheostomy. This is where I make an incision into her trachea, so that she may breathe through the hole which is created in her neck, while we work on removing that ball." With the owner's permission, I rushed Chelsea back to our treatment room.

"This is a critical," I told the techs with an edge in my voice to let them know that I was serious. Most critical patients are not standing and looking around like Chelsea, giving a false sense that she was okay. The technicians took my tone seriously. All attention was focused on

Chelsea. We placed an IV catheter to give us quick access to a vein which then allows us to deliver the anesthetic. I clipped the fur from her neck in case I needed to perform the tracheostomy. If the ball slipped backward during the extraction, it would only take a few short minutes to deprive her brain of oxygen.

I grabbed the instruments which I hoped would enable me to grasp the slick ball and I rapidly induced Chelsea under anesthesia. I recognized that anesthetizing her could cause the tissues in her throat to relax and possibly cut off any air that was currently able to bypass the ball. As quickly as possible, I passed a sharp needle with a thick suture through the rubber so I had an anchor in case it slipped. I wedged my fingers behind the ball, while Nancy, my technician, pulled on the attached line. In doing so, the ball successfully popped forward from her throat. We all breathed a sigh of relief. When Chelsea awoke, she immediately started wiggling exuberantly like the happy Standard Poodle that she should be. Big grins appeared on everyone's faces and we high-fived each other like jubilant teenagers. Walking into the waiting room, I bounced the small rubber racquetball over to the relieved owners. "I think a larger ball might be a better choice for her next playtime," I told them with a smile.

Not all dogs with this problem are so lucky. On a July 4th afternoon a man rushed in with a limp Scottish terrier nestled in his arms. There was a crowd of adults and children accompanying him.

"This is Mandy. Please save her," the man said in the waiting room, pushing his dog into my arms. I rushed her to the prep room, but Mandy was cold and stiff and her pupils were fixed and dilated. It was obvious that we would not be able to help her. I come back to the room to tell them the sad news. Through tears they relayed how they threw a piece of steak to her while they were picnicking on their patio. They said she was choking but I found this hard to believe. Most dogs will readily tear a piece of steak into manageable pieces. I pried open poor Mandy's frozen mouth and peered down with a focused light. Sure enough, wedged tightly in the opening of her larynx was a large hunk of meat. *That poor family*, I thought. I couldn't imagine the horror of throwing my beloved pet a snack in the midst of a festive barbeque to then have my family watch her asphyxiate to death.

Drug overdoses are not just confined to the human medical field. We also see drug over-doses with relative frequency in veterinary hospitals. On one of my ER shifts I entered the room to find two older teenagers impatiently waiting with their puppy, Max. Max was most definitely not normal. His head and eyes were tremoring profusely and any motion in his direction made him jump back in an abnormally hyperaesthetic motion. He circled and fell over and then stood up again and attempted, futilely, to circle once again. A short time later Max started to dribble urine. This was the last clue that I needed. It is the one clinical sign that does not mimic any other toxicity. In an attempt to be diplomatic, I queried the boys about all the things he could have gotten into – chocolate, caffeine, cigarettes, medications, antifreeze, or compost.

"No, no, no" was their response to each question that I asked.

"Any chance he could have gotten into some marijuana?" I smoothly slipped in at the end.

Here is your big chance to help your pet, I thought to myself. The boys looked nervous, but wouldn't admit to anything. This time, however, I noticed that the word, "No," was not coming from their mouths. I tried again, sticking with my hunch.

"I really don't care if you have pot," I told them "but for the sake of Max I need to know how to best care for him."

Again there was silence. I hospitalized Max and treated him based on my suspicions. I placed him on fluids and sedatives to control his severe tremors. He responded nicely and was back to being a playful dog the next day. I told Max, who was the equivalent of a teenager in dog years that if this occurred again I would be forced to send him for substance abuse counseling.

"Do you know what caused this?" asked the boy's mother who picked Max up the next day and paid their bill.

"Nope, not for sure, some unknown toxin," I replied truthfully. I suspected if those boys were smoking pot they would be a little more careful about where they stored it in the future.

It's not just teenagers that get their pets into trouble. More often than not it's a responsible adult. An older man arrived clutching his toy poodle to his chest.

"She can't stand," he told me worriedly "and she keeps falling over."

I examined her closely. Besides having a high-intensity heart murmur she seemed a bit droopy and unsteady. "We might want to run a few tests on her Mr. James to figure out what is going on," I said. When Mr. James saw the estimate, he decided to come clean with what had happened. He must have realized that, as embarrassing as it was, the truth would be cheaper than all the tests I would need to do to properly determine what was wrong with his poodle.

"We were having a party. She likes pina coladas. She only sipped from a few drinks. Do you think that could have done this, Doc?" he asked sheepishly.

I smiled as I thought to myself. *Yes, Mr. James. It is quite likely your frail little poodle with the heart condition is schnockered and that is why she is falling over. Now wasn't that easy.*

CHAPTER 7

KITTIES AND CLAWS

I was attempting to look at the scratched eye of a cat who was quietly sitting on my exam room table, when the cat seized the first opportunity it could to unexpectedly bolt. Rather than choosing his escape around me he chose his path over the top of me. He climbed up me and grabbed at my sweater front punching his nail tips into the skin of my chest and neck as he climbed. I felt his claws rip into my shoulder and then continue their damage as he moved down my back. Halfway down my back he paused, seemingly to survey his situation. I also stood motionless, overwhelmed with pain, and frantically trying to weigh my options. The thing was on my back, and blindly grabbing at him would likely end with me getting bit. The cat continued his slow course inching his way towards the floor which accelerated my thought process. Immediate action was necessary. The only solution that came to my mind was the response that I was taught as a child if I was on fire...the technique known as: "Stop, Drop and Roll." Well, my back was on fire from burning hot kitty claws, and dropping and rolling sounded like a great idea to me.

The cat's owners, a middle aged couple, looked on in surprise as I disappeared underneath the exam table. I fell over and rolled back and forth on the floor in an embarrassing attempt to extract the thing from my hide. The couple sat silently and wide eyed, watching my bizarre antics, not fully comprehending the reason why their veterinarian was rolling around on the exam room floor. Fortunately for my screaming skin, my rogue technique worked and the frightened kitty scampered off across the floor of the exam room looking for a less hazardous escape route than the one he had chosen. Later my technicians told me that all they heard from the opposite side of the door was "kitty, kitty, kitty" followed by a loud thud.

"You never knew that Stop, Drop and Roll was an effective restraint method, did you?" I said with a sour grin to my giggling technicians when I emerged from the room. They found it less amusing when I lifted the back of my shirt and showed them the raw red marks criss-crossing my back.

Mean cats are much less subtle and much more difficult to deal with than mean dogs. When cats are angry they arch their backs, flatten their ears, raise their fur, lift their tails, scream, yowl and lash at you with their claws…effectively disconcerting behaviors when you are confined in a small room with them. When cats are really mad they will scream as loud as they can and lunge at you in an attempt to unnerve you or to scare you off. Most will not actually complete the lunge to the point of making contact, these are just meant as warnings, but a few will not stop until their teeth have sunk into their targeted body part. With dogs, regardless of how mean or how aggressive they are, the fight is quickly over with the simple placement of a muzzle. You can attempt to muzzle cats but keeping the muzzle from slipping over their tiny round heads can be difficult if not impossible. Cats also have four sets of razor sharp claws located outside the safety of a muzzle which, when used, can cause significant bodily damage.

Drawing a blood sample from an uncooperative cat is always an adventure. In theory it should be easy…locate the large vein in their neck, bend your needle, stick it in the vein parallel to their neck and with a steady hand slowly pull back until your syringe is full. Now try it with a ten pound ball of feline fury – eyes dilated, claws protracted, tensing so much that the technician can barely raise the cat's head. It is growling ominously at you, with its face only inches from your face as you prepare for the needle stick. When you finally do penetrate its skin with the needle, the spawn of Satan screams at the top of its lungs and leaps off the table leaving you and your technicians to retrieve from whatever object it has found to crawl beneath.

We then call in a second tech for additional help. One tech to hold the front end and one to hold the back end. No such luck, by now the cat is lurching and jerking to such a degree that its vein is a moving target. We wrap it in what is called a kitty burrito. The kitty burrito is a technique where the uncooperative animal is rolled up into a towel with all four of its legs bundled within the towel. All that is left is a roll of a towel with a wide-eyed head and neck emerging from the end of it. Despite this, the cat is still intermittently able to get a paw out, often resulting in deep red lines across our hands. Hard to believe, but this ten pound animal is getting the best of the three of us. The real trick in drawing blood from a fractious cat is to draw the blood before it actually has time to wind up. Or better yet, avoid the whole scene by having the owner give it a sedative before it arrives. Better living through drugs can apply to veterinary medicine as well as human medicine.

Veterinarians also have restraint options for cats who are too aggressive to touch. One option is a device called a squeeze box. This is a plastic box where one of the walls is mobile, allowing you to gently confine the cat into a smaller and smaller space once it is inside of the box. There are holes in the outer walls made for injecting a sedative into the cat once it is tightly compressed within the box. An alternative method for sedating a fractious cat is an anesthetic chamber. This box is designed with connecting ports on the top of the box which fit to the hoses of a gas anesthetic machine. Once the ball of fury is slid into the box we can then pump the anesthetic gas into the chamber. We then happily watch as the aggressive ball of fur goes peacefully to sleep...just as we like him.

Encounters with aggressive animals are stressful situations for everyone involved. One day an owner arrived at our clinic carrying a carrier which was visibly shaking as the cat contained within its walls lunged from side to side of the box trying to get at whomever it could visualize through the small slats in the carrier's side. Since all it needed was a single vaccine we thought we would attempt a quick restraint with an oversized blanket and then give it the injection. The angry cat was quickly dumped out of the carrier and onto the table and I threw a thick blanket over its head and body to contain it. I found myself holding a hissing, shrieking, thirteen pound ball of muscle beneath the blanket. It was taking all of my strength to keep it there. The strength of an angry feline never fails to amaze me.

"Give the vaccine in its butt," I told Kathy, a seasoned technician who was standing nearby and who wasn't easily intimidated by screaming, aggressive cats.

I couldn't see what was happening, but I could feel Kathy lifting the blanket near the back end of the oscillating mass and attempting to find the correct anatomic location to place the vaccine. Precisely at that moment something happened which stopped my heart cold. First, a loud yowl filled the room, and then what felt like a muscular yet fuzzy creature leaped onto my back. Two paws surrounded my head, followed by a firm whack, whack, whack, as I was forcefully boxed across my ears and face. I was certain that the screaming, gnashing beast which a minute ago had been safely contained beneath the blanket in my hands, had somehow slipped out and was now sitting on my shoulders trying to macerate me.

"Get him off me!" I yelled terrified.

And then, just as quickly as it had leaped on, the creature jumped off my shoulders. Through the corner of my eyes I could see a black and white blur fleeing rapidly from the room. I looked down and reassured myself that the fierce cat that I had been holding was still tucked away beneath the blanket. The cat was still there but it was now eerily silent and I sensed a tone of submissiveness. I'm sure this clever cat was wisely thinking that it should remain covert under the blanket until the crazy beast out there was gone.

"What in the hell's name is going on?" I asked trying hard to regain my composure. Everyone in the room was bent over shaking with laughter. I failed to see the humor in the situation.

"That was the clinic cat." they informed me with tears welling from their eyes.

The clinic cat who lived at the hospital was obviously not impressed with the restraint techniques that I had used on my patient. I can only presume that she must have been a distant relative of the cat that I was vaccinating. She had taken it upon herself to jump on my back and reprimand me for what she must have seen as improper treatment of her guest. The sheer terror of the moment, followed by the relief that I felt when I realized that I had just been ambushed by a docile and declawed hospital cat, also left me rolling with laughter. As scary as that moment was, I would take that any day from having the cat from hell slashing at my face from on top of my shoulders.

CHAPTER 8

YES, I CAN

etting into veterinary school is notoriously difficult. Many students aspire to be veterinarians and the strong application field makes for stiff competition. In order to be eligible you need to have high grades, a strong work ethic, and the perseverance to finish a long and difficult education process. There are only thirty veterinary schools in the United States, not even one per state, and there is an average of eighty students per class. To be accepted you need a high grade point average, and high scores on your college admission tests. You will also need to demonstrate an interest in the field by working a prerequisite number of hours in an animal related industry, or at a veterinary practice. Only after you have fulfilled these requirements do you become an eligible candidate for veterinary school.

High school guidance counselors warn prospective applicants that the chances of being accepted to veterinary school are relatively slim. I applied to six schools hoping that I would get accepted to at least one of them. Most of the schools asked only for a written application, but a few recommended a physical on-site interview with the admission board members. To maximize my chances of acceptance I flew to the universities that requested this of me.

One interview at a veterinary school was particularly memorable. It was on a cold, winter Saturday at a university in a northeastern state, I found myself in a windowless room in front of five grim-faced professors, all who seemed to have scowls imprinted on their faces. They were lined up in a row behind a cafeteria style table. They were all gray-haired and most of them were spectacled. Not one of them showed a hint of a smile or offered me an encouraging word. The meeting had been scheduled for a Friday, but instead it was happening on a Saturday, as my connecting flight had been delayed. I was sure that having to be on campus on their day off was not helping their level of grumpiness or my chances for acceptance to their program. After brief introductions, they began to fire off a series of questions in monotone voices.

This group quizzed me first on basic biology facts, and then proceeded to questions regarding my knowledge of some of the more recent developments in veterinary medicine. I was able to answer most of these with little difficulty. I was surprised and impressed when they went off the normal course of questioning and asked me to explain the composition and design of a snow ski. I had indicated in my application that skiing was one of the extracurricular sports that I enjoy. I thought it was clever. It was their way of making me demonstrate my personal knowledge and level of curiosity about the technicalities and mechanics of a subject in which I had expressed enthusiasm.

Their next interview question gave me pause.

"How do you know that you are capable of handling an emergency situation?" one spectacle wearing round faced man asked. "Not everyone is capable of dealing with the stress and emotions and quick thinking that are necessary in an emergency situation. Do you think that you're capable of handling that?"

I knew that I looked like a soft, naive college kid who wouldn't have the gumption to handle the blood, gore, and charged emotions which were present in a true emergency situation. I sat quietly thinking and then answered them as honestly as I could, knowing that they probably weren't prepared for the answer that they would get. People usually don't want to hear the truth, particularly if an answer digs down to the blackest depths of a person's soul.

"I'm pretty sure I can handle the emotions and stresses of a critical emergency if it occurs. Yes, sir, I can." I said this with a quiet confidence that belied my age.

They waited for me to go on, I was skeptical that there was any one single answer that would convince them with certainty.

"I once was involved in a critical emergency in my own life and I did just fine. And in fact it was partly what inspired me to want to go into a medical field. With that particular incident I saw how a team of people can work together calmly and cohesively to get the job done as smoothly and as quickly as the situation allows."

I relayed the story that had occurred five years earlier in the back yard of my own home. It was a story I rarely told anyone, as the telling of it usually brought me to tears. It was a quiet, muggy day in August. It was the summer between my sophomore and junior year at college and I was working as a cashier at a local supermarket. I was upstairs trying to nap before my evening shift. A loud frantic knocking at my front door startled me awake. I lived in an isolated area and our house was perched up high on a steep hill. It was rare to have visitors at our door. I went downstairs in my pajamas thinking that it must be my step-dad who had locked himself outside once again. I opened the door to find a frail, elderly man standing there. He appeared white-faced and frazzled.

"There's a woman down on the street and she's trapped under a car," he stuttered out.

"What are you talking about?" I answered confused by his unexpected and seemingly irrational statement.

"A woman, she's under the car at the bottom of the hill," he said this time with more insistence.

"What kind of car?" I asked suddenly suspicious of his intentions. I was a young girl alone in a remote neighborhood. Maybe he was just trying to lure me outside. Maybe I shouldn't have answered the door.

"A black Subaru. It's in the woods. She's trapped under the car and she's yelling." He wasn't waiting for my reply. He turned around and started a fast hobble down the walkway gesturing for me to follow him. I started after him barefoot and in my pajamas. My footsteps quickened as some of the possibilities swirled around in my head.

At the top of our driveway it registered that my mother's Subaru was no longer parked in its usual spot. My eyes swept down the steep asphalt driveway, and at the far bottom of the hill I could see her black sedan parked askew with its tail in the woods and its nose just emerging onto the road. While I was surveying the scene a car drove slowly by. The driver glanced at the oddly parked car, and then continued on his way home. I ran down the hill toward the car, gaining momentum as I went, with a heightened sense of panic as I got closer. The elderly gentleman shuffled behind me as quickly as he was able. I didn't have the faintest idea of what had happened, but I could see skid marks across the road and I recognized one of my mother's sneakers lying on the asphalt near the edge of the road.

I ran to the car pushing away shrubbery as I fell onto my knees to peer under. The sight that I was viewing a few inches from my face stopped me cold. My mother was lying trapped under the body of the car. She was folded at the waist with her face pressed into the dirt and one leg seemed skewed in an odd direction. The underbody of the car seemed to be digging into her back and was compressing her forcefully into the ground.

"Laura, help me," she gasped in a weak, terrified voice.

"Mom, Mom," I croaked. I felt helpless. I pulled away the brush from around her head and tried to clear some of the dirt from her mouth.

"Get....help," she whispered, her words were coming out in gasps. Slow, stilted and frightened words.

"I'll be right back," I said standing up. I had to run back up the long driveway to find the nearest phone.

"Stay there," I told her realizing immediately what a ridiculous thing that was to say. I turned away with a sick feeling in my stomach, fighting a strong urge not to leave her alone. I ran as fast as I could up the steep driveway, threw open the door and ran to the kitchen where the phone was located. I got on the telephone and frantically dialed 911.

"Police," said a bored voice over the receiver.

"My mother is trapped under a car at the bottom of our driveway," I gasped, breathing heavily from the run.

"Your mother is trapped under a car?" the female voice repeated slowly and mechanically as if trying to insure that she had not misheard me.

"Yes," I yelled loudly "Please send help." I spelled out our address rapidly.

"I need you to return to the scene of the accident and confirm again that there is a woman trapped under a car," the mechanical sounding operator said to me in a disbelieving voice.

You must be fucking kidding me ran through my mind as a reply, but instead knowing that time was precious, I quietly but intensely replied, "My mother is under a car, she's trapped under the car. I confirmed it when I saw her there the first time. Send help now."

I gave them the address and slammed the handle onto the receiver with force. My hands were now starting to shake. I ran back down to the car praying my mom was still conscious. I lay down in the dirt and wedged myself under the car so that I was lying beside her and reached for her hand which felt cold and limp. I kept talking to her in a calm voice…a constant jabber of words designed to reassure her that everything was just fine. I told her that help was coming quickly and that we would be out of here in a jiffy. We lay together under the car in the unbearable heat and waited for what seemed like an interminable amount of time until in the distance I could hear the sweetest sound ever…the sound of a siren which was getting louder and louder as it approached our block.

"It's okay, Mom, they're almost here, they are going to help."

I refused to let panic or fear creep into my voice. I knew that for my mother's sake I needed to stay calm. My mother had stopped answering me which was internally escalating my panic but I could still feel the light rhythmic movement of her sides reassuring me that she was breathing.

A face peered under the chassis and I was unceremoniously jerked from under the car by large hands. A group of policemen were working together to clear the brush and dirt from around the car and yelling directions to each other. I sat in the middle of the road watching the ongoing chaos. A circle of my neighbors gathered and one large woman pulled me over to the group and tightly clutched me to her bosom.

I heard one of the policemen explain to another what had happened. The Subaru had rolled from the top of the driveway, past numerous large trees on the lawn and then went over the final steep drop where my mother had been weeding the roadside garden. It hit her head-on without any warning sounds, as its engine was off. Grabbing her with its undercarriage, it dragged her across the asphalt. It then landed in the woods with her lodged beneath. I heard one of my neighbors say he had seen the car more than an hour ago when he drove home from work, and had mused on what an odd place it was to have been parked. Car after car after car had passed the misplaced Subaru and not one had bothered to stop.

"Don't look, don't look," my matronly well-meaning neighbor kept saying as she hugged me tight to her body in an attempt to prevent me from watching my mother's final extraction. My neighbor wouldn't let go despite my protests. I wanted, needed to know what was happening. That was my mother under there, and I was more than aware that she might shortly be dead. But regardless, I wanted to see what was happening…to know what she looked like when they were finally able to lift the car off of her…to see if I could help her or comfort her. I was more than okay with seeing my mother in whatever condition she emerged, as long as she was still breathing when they did so. I pushed my neighbor off and walked back to the car.

The car was elevated off of my mother with large airbags. Her tiny, limp body with a pale, white face and bloody tattered clothes was gently slid from beneath the car onto a board. The waiting paramedics placed large tubular balloons around her legs and arms, in an effort to force her blood flow back to the core of her body. One was working with intense concentration to place an IV line in her arm while the other one held an oxygen mask over her face. I heard them announce into the walkie-talkie that her blood pressure was reading 40. Even I knew that was a terribly low number. They started hurriedly wheeling her into the ambulance.

I ran over, pushing off the grabbing arms of the officers. Her eyes were closed and she seemed lifeless. Her hand was clammy and cold in mine. Her face and hair were smeared with dirt and twigs. She wasn't responding anymore and she had stopped moving.

"Mom, I love you," I whispered to her. "Hold on, you're going to be okay." But I was feeling less and less sure of my words.

My mom did survive the episode and my family survived the heartbreaking, painful, and prolonged recovery. She spent more than three months in a hospital with eighteen broken bones, punctured lungs, internal hemorrhaging, and a large portion of her back skinned off from where the car had dragged her across the asphalt. She had numerous surgeries, months of wound care, a tentative skin graft, and years of a painful and debilitating recovery. Her recovery left her with a permanent limp and permanent pain, but even worse, she lost the feisty fearlessness that I had always known from her. Forever after she seemed fearful, timid and afraid to try anything new...a pale shadow of the person that I had once known.

Finishing my story without shedding a tear, I glanced up at the stodgy and now uncomfortable appearing board members. I looked them in the eyes and told them again with confidence that I knew that I was more than capable of handling any emergency in a veterinary hospital. In fact I was an initiated expert. I think this time, they wholeheartedly believed me and their questioning ceased. The interview ended shortly after that. I did not get accepted to their university but I was placed on the waiting list.

My mother's accident focused my life in several ways. It gave me the knowledge and confidence that I could handle whatever was thrown my way in life. It reaffirmed that I wanted to pursue a career in medicine, and that I was capable of handling the stress and emotions that comes with dealing with medical emergencies. I had stayed calm and collected in the face of a personal nightmare. I had also spent long hours in a hospital that year. I was fascinated by the environment of a hospital and all the medical procedures. I observed my mother's resuscitation efforts at the emergency room, the teams of doctors working together to stabilize her, and afterwards, the teams of surgical and rehabilitative doctors working together to make her better. I wanted to be a part of that world and discover how I could learn to help injured beings.

A terrible, frightening tragedy happened to my family and we all made it through the ordeal. It bonded us in a way that few other things could. In an equally powerful way it had awakened me to a true under standing of how fragile and tentative life really is. Common clichés that once seemed trivial suddenly had a real and relatable meaning for me. There is a reason why these clichés have survived over all this time. It's because they have proven themselves time after time to be meaningful if you really pay attention to what they are saying. Don't sweat the small stuff. Live your life to the fullest. Cherish the people that you love. Listen to your heart, follow your dreams and enjoy the journey.

As it turns out I now had my own personal life cliché to follow.

Live your life to its fullest right now, because you never know when a car is going to roll down a hill and hit you while you're gardening.

The terror that I experienced that day branded itself deeply onto my heart, and I have spent the rest of my life refusing to deviate from the understanding that I developed on and after that fateful day. My life was going to be my own and I was never going to let anything, not my job, not my family, not society, dissuade me from experiencing everything that I wanted to conquer or experience in life.

Life is way too short and way too unpredictable to do anything else.

CHAPTER 9

SEX

A one-year-old Pomeranian was rushed into our hospital weak, limp and not moving. The dog's heart rate was a barely obtainable twenty-eight beats per minute and we were working intensely to help him. He was in the end stages of shock, which is the stage closest to death. We placed an intravenous line, gave him fluids, placed an oxygen mask on him and infused medications designed to increase the heart's contractility abilities and rate. We placed a warmer, which looks like a giant blow dryer and is used to raise the temperature, to blow warm air under the blankets covering him. Fifteen minutes later the Jack Russell puppy was sitting up and looking around weakly. If I were to anthropomorphize, I would say the dog's expression was somewhere between astonished to end up in a strange room with a group of strangers staring over him, and grateful that he was still alive. I gave the pup a pat and walked into the exam room to talk with his worried owners.

"I think your pup's going to be okay with time, but we nearly lost her." I told the relieved looking owners.

The husband looked at me and responded, "He's a boy, not a girl," and then without cracking a smile added: "Are you really a doctor?"

I was a bit taken aback. First, by his tone which didn't sound as if he was joking and second, for his lack of gratitude for my help. I had just worked intensely to save his young dog. A dog who just a few minutes before had been dying in front of us and who was now sitting up and looking around the room because of the skilled efforts of my team. This was a funny way of showing appreciation. *I guess I was just so busy trying to save HIS life that I wasn't paying attention to what genitals HE had,* I replied to myself, just so my childish desires to be the last person to speak could be fulfilled. I ignored his remark and directed the conversation in a more productive way, explaining what I felt was wrong with their critically ill pup, and what we needed to do next.

Owners are usually not shy about making us aware of their pet's correct gender. It seems to be a form of verbal proof to them that our skills and knowledge as a veterinarian are up to par.

"It's a he," they will intercept if I inadvertently use the word, "she" while I'm explaining to them what we need to do to get their dog out of heart failure. *Okay,* I want to say, *now let's focus on what's really important about this conversation, which is that your dog is in our back room's oxygen chamber slowly dying from the fluid which is filling up his lungs. We can continue to discuss this point of what sex he is, which will be fairly irrelevant to his her or her outcome, but every minute will count here in trying to help your dog.*

Veterinarians have a little trick of making the front sheet of their record pink or blue so that in a quick glance they can tell the pet's gender. This helps to avoid embarrassing mistakes that may anger an owner. Another trick of the trade is to use genderless, generic terms of endearment such as "honey" or "sweetheart" that will avoid any chance of owner irritation if we happen to forget what sex their pet is while looking at its mouth.

For a while I was dubbed "The Penis Doctor" by my technician, Donna, because I seemed to be the attending doctor every time an animal with a penis problem came into the clinic. Dogs get a medical problem called a paraphimosis (para-fim-osis). This is a condition where their penis enlarges to such an extent that they are unable to replace it back into the sheath. The sheath is the protective structure that anatomically covers their penis.

The poor dog suffering from this condition arrives at our hospital with his penis distended, swollen, and purple in color. If it is left in this state for a long enough period, the penis will start to lose blood supply and the traumatized skin of the penis will devitalize and slough off in sheets of thin tissue. The miserable dog now gets to endure the embarrassment of three unknown medical personnel actively working to reduce the size of his swollen and diseased penis. If manual compression of the structure does not work we will then make a last ditch effort which is to pour thickened sugar water onto the penis. The theory behind this technique is that the sugar is supposed to have an osmotic pull which reduces the swelling by drawing the fluid from his penis. Coating the poor fellow's penis in sugar mash does little to restore the dog's dignity but at least has the advantage of providing tasty licking material for him afterwards. If these medical interventions fail to help, then a surgical incision will need to be made into the overlying sheath to widen its opening. This usually solves the problem. After a month where several paraphimosis wielding dogs arrived at our hospital, followed by an incident where an errant BB shot lodged itself within a dog's penis which I subsequently had to surgically extract, I officially earned and accepted my title as the Penis Doctor.

As veterinary students, we are taught all kinds of odd facts about animal penises. I am now eternally enlightened with the quintessential knowledge that boars have cork screw shaped penises, and tomcats have small barbs on the ends of their penises which magically disappear after they are neutered. The evolutionary function of those barbs, which seem a bit masochistic to the average woman contemplating their purpose, remains a mystery to biologists. Waterfowl have a penis which when exposed in its everted state takes up twenty-five percent of the length of its body. Dogs have an actual bone which runs through the center of their penis, which quite unimaginatively is called an Os Penis. One classmate of mine who had a quirky sense of fashion converted a pair of Os Penis' into earrings. Admittedly, veterinarians as a whole are a bit odd.

Testicles, unlike the rest of the business world, are also a routine part of a veterinarian's daily conversation. As vets we all do everything that we can to encourage owners to spay and neuter their dogs and cats. There is a huge overpopulation of pets in the United States. This means that we need to regularly educate owners about their animal's testicles, and why we feel that their pet should part with these particular body parts. Male owners, for obvious reasons, seem much more attached to their pet's testicles than female owners. Interestingly, men seem to take more offense to having their dog's testicles removed than they do to having their cat's testicles removed. My suspicion is that this is because dogs strut their stuff with their bits hanging proudly on display for the world to see. Cat's testicles are anatomically different looking, they are furry, hidden, and tucked well beneath them. They are just a little less human-looking than a dog's testicles. Men, understandably, seem to empathize with the pain that their dogs will experience, their secondary concern seems to relate to the loss of masculinity they perceive their dog will experience. Overall, the women are less sympathetic and, more often than not, it is the wife who shows up on surgery day eagerly handing their dog over to us for his little "procedure."

Semen collection is another valuable skill that veterinarians are required to learn in veterinary school...a skill which my male acquaintances seem to think is just groovy. The semen in dogs is collected using a manual technique. My reproduction professor, would recount the story of how she had to collect repetitive semen samples from a dog for a research project. Apparently this dog liked the manual method just a little too much. He would take every opportunity to escape, make his way through the expansive hallways of the hospital, and then shamelessly sit at her office door waiting for his perceived sweetheart's return.

In veterinary school, we are also taught collection techniques of farm animals, such as bulls or stallions, so that the semen can be stored for purposes of artificial insemination. Artificial insemination is a huge and profitable industry in this country, catering to the beef and dairy cattle farms, the swine industry, the breeding horse farms and the dog breeding industry. In school my friend, Kelly, was the student picked to demonstrate for the class how to collect semen from a stallion using an AV. An AV is the slang abbreviation in the veterinary world for an artificial vagina. Wearing a hard hat for protection, Kelly had to walk under the belly of a powerful stallion who was mounting a dummy mare. From this position Kelly was instructed to collect the stallion's semen. Kelly relayed later that all she could see was a giant penis forcefully waving towards her head as she attempted to place the AV into the correct position. Flipping her long blond hair with a coy smile, she remarked that the professor had told her that she had collected semen in record time that day.

Unbeknownst to the general public, stallions have another more natural way of expressing their sexuality than attempted copulations with a hapless veterinary student. They masturbate. Walking down the aisle of a stable housing a stallion, one might hear an out-of-sorts noise. Something like whack, whack, whack. That is the not-so-surreptitious sound of a stallion masturbating. They take their distended penis and rhythmically hit it against their underbelly to masturbate. I'm assuming that this is pleasurable for them. These guys aren't hiding a "Playhorse" magazine under their hay manger but more likely are responding to a mare nearby who is in estrus and whose hormones are particularly potent that evening. In similar fashion, my old college roommate confided in me that their Labrador, Sam, would passionately start humping his pillow if she and her husband were in a particularly heated moment. Usually when a dog is humping an object it is a dominant behavior but I was having a hard time explaining why Sam would suddenly start making love to his pillow only when his owner's pheromones were exuding so strongly.

In high school I watched in sick fascination as the only tomcat in the Persian cattery where I worked, positioned himself over a rug that he had carefully rolled up in an accommodating shape and then proceeded to try to mate with new his carpet friend. The cat was the only male in a room composed entirely of female cats and he spent most of his day confined to a large screened-in cage in the middle of the room. The females who had free run of the room would walk by his cage, bat their eyelashes and lift their well fluffed tails as they rubbed against his cage. The poor tormented fellow rarely had any other recourse except his buddy, the well-worn carpet in his cage.

The other type of sex is also prevalent in the veterinary world. This is partly due to the fact that we are a profession that is immersed in a world which uses the terms urine and feces and penises and uteruses on a regular basis. The casual and isolated atmosphere of a veterinary hospital, along with the subjects we routinely deal with, is fertile ground for inappropriate remarks. For this reason, overt incidences of inappropriate remarks or actions occur fairly commonly behind the closed doors of veterinary hospitals...perhaps more frequently than in other businesses. "Jingle balls, Jingle Balls, Jingle all the way," sang a technician named Tasha in a cheery, loud voice down the hallway. The song was a response to our shift leader complaining that one of the ER doctors had agreed to neuter a cat on Christmas Eve after she fixed the laceration the owner had found on his shoulder. "Who the hell schedules a neuter on Christmas Eve anyway?" lamented Lana when the doctor wasn't around to hear her complain. Merry Christmas Kitty.

At one hospital where I had regular relief work, I got some unwelcome attention from a male technician. He was a legal immigrant from an Eastern bloc country. My previous experiences with men from this region of the world were that they tended to be a bit machismo. He had a tendency of telling sexually oriented jokes, or making off-colored comments. In the past I had ignored his mildly offensive remarks and tried to write it off as a cultural difference in communicating. On this particular day his comments seemed more vulgar and inappropriate than usual. We were anesthetizing an animal to do a dental cleaning when I asked him to pass the anesthesia hose.

"You want my hose," he drawled in his heavily accented voice as he squeezed past me within the tight confines where we were working. He stopped when he was in a position directly behind me and mumbled a comment about enjoying this spot. Anger welled up inside of me, but just at that moment the front door clanged, signaling a client's arrival at the hospital. I had to redirect my attention to her.

The final straw came later that afternoon. I was wearing a short white lab coat over my pants. It came to just below my waist. I turned to walk away from Vito and he commented that I should be careful as he believed I was gaining weight. Now this was a double indemnity. First, having the nerve to comment on my weight and second, having no qualms that the only thing he could possibly have been viewing as I walked away from him was my ass. Now I was pissed. Hell hath no fury like a woman whose ass is critiqued as being too large.

As a temporary employee at this hospital I was a guest. I knew that any direct remarks would not have any lasting repercussions. Yet Vito had a crossed a line that required the higher powers above me. This situation required the intervention of his manager. The next day I approached the manager with explicit descriptions of his past comments and behaviors. I was hesitant. I relied on this relief position as a major source of my income and I did not want to rock any boats. I also knew that Vito's behavior was unacceptable and repetitive. The work environment had become intolerable for me. To my relief, Terry, the hospital's manager, was not dismissive at all. Instead she listened with interest and took notes. I had the feeling that it wasn't the first time that she had caught wind of such news. The next time I returned, Vito no longer worked at that hospital. I felt bad, but only for a short time. Vito's bad behavior had continued for far too long and he had been given more than one chance for redemption. Although being laid off is a severe consequence, ultimately he had chosen his own path.

CHAPTER 10

X-RAY VISION

I have knowledge and insight about animals that the average pet owner does not have. I can see their pet's future, and with the use of my hands and my eyes and my ears I can see inside of them. I have x-ray vision. And sometimes that works to my advantage, but sometimes I hate having the gift.

A good friend of mine called me up one Sunday morning while I was at work. "Kayla isn't acting right," he said. "She didn't eat this morning and she seems quieter than normal."

It all sounded fairly benign. My dog doesn't eat at every feeding and we all have quiet moments. Still, any change in normal behavior in your pet, should prompt a veterinary exam by the owner.

"Bring her down if you'd like, James," I said. "I would be happy to take a look at her."

James and Kayla arrived a short time later. As soon as I walked into the exam room I knew something was wrong. Kayla was standing and looking around the room, but she seemed more reserved than normal. She was not the happy, interactive, bouncing dog that I was used to seeing. Usually she would greet me enthusiastically, wag her tail unendingly, and stare at me with big soulful eyes until I took the time to say hello to her. Today her eyes had a dull glaze that worried me.

She was a great dog. I had known her for several years. I had spent time with her camping and hiking, and had been on rafting trips with her. She had been to our house many times for dinner parties or watching movies. She was everything that an owner could want in a pet – intelligent, kind, gentle, playful and athletic. James was a consummate bachelor, and she was James' constant companion and friend. She went everywhere with him and he would turn down opportunities to go places just so that he didn't have to leave her behind.

I started my exam on Kayla. Her gum color was pale pink rather than a healthy raspberry pink. Her heart rate was elevated for how sluggish she appeared, and when I felt her belly, it felt swollen and doughy. My heart sank, I knew immediately what was going on and that this was going to be very, very bad. As I looked at James I was trying to look calm, trying hard to keep the expression of fear off of my face.

"Let me take her in the back so I can do a few tests," I said trying to act nonchalant. I wanted to get a quick ultrasound of her belly to confirm my suspicions before I ruined James' day and changed how the rest of his life would play out.

"Okay," he casually replied.

The pleasant expression on his face indicated to me that he did not have a clue how concerned I was, which was exactly how I wanted it right then. My heart ached for him. I knew that Kayla had a terrible disease and that she may not be alive in a few short hours. I didn't want to do the ultrasound, didn't want to confirm what I believed to be true. I wanted blissful ignorance as well.

The ultrasound affirmed my suspicions. Kayla had what we call in medical terminology a hemoabdomen. In lay-man's terms this translates into "a belly full of blood". A condition which has occurred because a tumor, which has been silently growing in her spleen for months, has ruptured on this particular day. Kayla was slowly bleeding to death in front of us. We could bring Kayla to surgery and remove her spleen, which would stop the hemorrhage, but, the statistics were stacked high that this type of tumor would be aggressive and would shortly spread to other organs in her body. The reality is that, even if James did pursue surgery, Kayla would only live a few short months afterwards.

Why did I get this case? Why didn't James and Kayla arrive on another night when a different doctor was working? I didn't want to tell James what I had just seen in the ultrasound room. I knew it would devastate him. He was single and unemployed, and Kayla was everything to him. Now I had to tell him that Kayla needed an emergency surgery which I knew he couldn't afford, and then I had to tell him that he had about an hour to make up his mind about the surgery before she bled to death. His choices at that moment were down to two, bring her to surgery or euthanize her. At that moment I hated my job. I wanted nothing more than to give it all up and work at McDonalds where my biggest concern would be how many sauces to hand out with the chicken nuggets.

I told James what was happening, trying the whole time to hold back my own tears. When I gave him the news he looked as if he was going to vomit. I felt as if I wanted to vomit too. James was my friend. Kayla was an amazing companion to him and a dog who brought intermittent joy to my life as well. It was one of the hardest things I have had to do in my veterinary career. I prayed that I wouldn't ever have to impart such awful and unexpected news to someone that I cared about again.

As I expected, James couldn't bring Kayla to surgery. Given the odds and the further stress and pain that surgery would place on his dog, I'm not sure that I would have chosen surgery for my dog either. James did get lucky at least in one way that day. The tumor in her spleen stopped bleeding on its own accord. Occasionally this happens to a lucky animal sparing the owner the horrific task of having to make any immediate decisions about the fate of their pet. I was thrilled that James would not have to make an instantaneous decision, like so many others are forced to do when they arrive at our hospital with a pet who is suffering from this same condition. The resorption of that blood from her belly back into her vascular system allowed Kayla to regain her strength back over the next few days. As it turns out James was exceptionally lucky. Most of the time, within the first week the tumor will start bleeding again quickly placing the pet back into an emergency situation. In Kayla's case she thrived for so long that James was able to spend a few more weeks with her. This allowed him to take her on a final camping trip and gave James the time that he needed to process her terminal disease and say a proper goodbye to his long term friend.

My x-ray vision allows me to know things about animals that I see on the streets. I hate it. I can't just take a nonchalant walk down the road. Instead I find myself diagnosing the medical problems of every dog that passes me. I notice a subtle limp on a ball-playing Labrador in the park and wonder if the owner has any idea that his dog has partially torn a ligament in his knee and is probably in discomfort when he runs. I stop to talk to a lady whose dog's eye looks wet and teary and who repeatedly blinks the lids of that eye. I want to tell her that her dog is constantly blinking because he has a painful condition where his lashes are ingrown. I don't. I'm not sure that she doesn't already know that it's a problem, or maybe she has consulted a vet already and has just chosen to ignore the issue, or perhaps she just doesn't care to know. I stop at the mall and pass by the pet store. I see a mother with three active boys cooing over a sad- faced Bassett puppy in a cage. *Don't do it*, I want to say. I know it is cute now but it's going to grow up to be goofy and oversized and unruly. It is going to have constant skin and ear problems and intermittent back problems too. It's going to be stubborn and lazy and it won't play with your children and because it is a hound dog, it won't listen to your boys when they give it commands. It is not the right dog for an athletic and active family. I know that it wouldn't matter if I did tell them. Their hearts are set on this now wrinkly and adorable puppy. They'll buy it, pay way too much for a pet store puppy, and won't know the difference until they realize how frequent the veterinary visits are or until they are repeatedly chasing after it, as it runs down the road pursuing every errant smell that it encounters.

Walking down my own street one day, I heard a grunt, grunt, grunt sound approaching me from far down the block. I knew exactly what it was from the sounds that I could hear. Every time I hear this noise within the walls of our hospital I cringe. It's a brachycephalic (braky-se-fall-ic) dog of some sort. Brachycephalic is just a fancy medical name for a dog with a smush-faced conformation such as a Boxer, or a Bull-dog, or a Pug. Every veterinary professional that I know can list a long litany of medical problems that come along with having a dog of that conformation. I hate that noise, as to me it represents a very cute animal who can't breathe properly. As an ER vet, who recognizes that breathing is an important requirement for living a normal and active life, I prefer to be around animals who can breathe normally. To me those sounds are not cute, it's torturous. These snorting and grunting noises are so loud because these dog's airways are compressed, in essence, with each breath they take they are struggling for air. This is a result of generations of careful trait-selective breeding and people's penchant for bizarrely cute looking animals.

Some of these dog's airways are so compromised that the only way they can obtain air is by holding their mouths open. This point was highlighted to me one day at my office when I had a young Boxer pass out on the exam room table after I placed a muzzle on her because she was being snippy. The simple act of forcing this Boxer to maintain her mouth closed for a few minutes resulted in her almost passing out in front of me. Normally built animals can readily breathe through their nostrils when a muzzle is placed on them, but this dog's nasal anatomy was so compressed that she was simply incapable of breathing with her mouth shut.

The grunting and huffing sound from down the street came closer. I got a visual on the sounds. It was a cute little Pug which already looked winded from its short walk. At least she was not obese. People will kill their pets with kindness by feeding them too much. This problem is exaggerated, in smush- faced breeds, as the extra fat acts to further compresses their already compromised airways.

The man stopped in front of me. Huff, huff, gasp, snort, gasp, snort. The dog sat down, glad to be able to stop and catch her breath.

"Cute dog," I told him, trying to be sociable with a neighbor. What I really wanted to do was ask how he could tolerate all of that endless noise in his home.

"That's Mitzy," the man informed me, and then for some reason felt the need to add, "she's an idiot. But she's the only idiot we have, and we love her."

He walked on, dragging the reluctant and snorting Mitzy behind him. Great, an idiot dog who can't breathe. I wish I had one too. I also wish that I didn't have to feel sorry for this animal. I just want to take a happy and peaceful walk. I want to be ignorant of what all those breathing noises really mean.

Sometimes I can see an animal's future. We were camping with a group of friends for the fourth of July. Everyone brought their dogs. James, was there with his newly adopted puppy named Scooter. An exuberant, friendly four-month-old golden cross. I was happy and excited for James. He had waited a long time before bringing a new dog into his life and he seemed content again. James is one of those people who always seems empty if he doesn't have a dog at his side. We set up our tents while the dogs all played on the beach in a mass frenzy. I looked up to watch the chaotic scene and as I did, Scooter ran by me. A sinking feeling developed in my chest. Scooter had that bunny-hopping gait that you can see with dogs who have hip dysplasia. Maybe it wasn't true. Maybe I was over interpreting the way that he moved, maybe he had a splinter in his toe. I told myself not to look at his gait and maybe the problem would go away. Nope, no such luck. A little while later, I saw Scooter running down the beach moving with that same funny gait.

Hip dysplasia is a dirty word to most people. It means your dog has a genetic abnormality of his hips that, which over time, will progress to debilitating arthritis. Sometimes it is subtle and only manifested by a dog's unwillingness to move or run. Other times it causes a severe pain that gives them a stiff gait or makes it difficult for them to rise or move around like a normal dog. Often it doesn't become clinically apparent to the owners until it is later in their dog's life, but the truth is the problem has been present since its birth. A diagnosis of this devastating orthopedic disease may mean that you will be medicating your dog for life or, for the more severely affected pups, a radical surgery to try and correct it.

I looked around at the six dogs playing in a group on the beach. I could find medical and behavioral issues in all of them if I watched long or closely enough. What's the difference, their owners love them and are completely oblivious to what I can see. I'm here on my vacation weekend. This is my respite from my work. James loves Scooter, and Scooter is here to stay no matter what medical problems he may have. Nothing I say is going to change that. If he wants my professional opinion, I'll give it to him. But I am not going to tell him unless he asks. Let him enjoy their bliss while it lasts, and this time I will let his family veterinarian be the bearer of any bad news.

CHAPTER II

THE INJUSTICES OF THE WORLD

When my mother was hit by an errant car I thought that nothing in my life could be as frightening. I thought that the worst scenario had happened to my family and we had overcome it together. As it turns out, I was wrong. Dead wrong. Worse things do happen. Several years later on a sunny Tuesday afternoon, on the second day of January, my father was instantaneously killed as a dump truck ran a red light and hit his van head on. This tragic accident set the tone for my New Year ahead.

My father was on his lunch hour returning back to his office. I was twenty-eight years old. I had graduated from veterinary school just a short time earlier. The evening before his death I spoke to my father for the last time. I cut the conversation short so that I could get to a movie. I had a new date and I did not want to be late. The next day while I was at work I received a phone call informing me of his death. That phone call, which lasted just a brief few minutes, and the interrupted conversation that I had with him the night before, has haunted my life ever since.

His unexpected and violent death left me with an unsettled feeling that I just could not shake. My life had become unglued again and my fright over the unpredictability of life returned with a vengeance that I could not control. I became terrified that my death would be next. Mostly, I was terrified that I was going to become permanently incapacitated or die before I had accomplished the goals and dreams that I had set for myself. If I was truly going to "live my life to its utmost capacity," then I had better get going and I should go at it at a much faster rate. I made a list of my dreams and my aspirations. On the top of my list was my desire to travel. I had traveled on short trips to foreign countries but I was yearning to travel for a more extended period. I wanted to immerse myself into the daily life of a foreign country and saturate myself in a foreign culture. In retrospect I realize that I was also looking to extract myself from the pain and the nightmare of the life that I was living.

A short time later it all fell into place. Stepping out from my fantasy wish list, a 6'1", blonde, blue-eyed, muscular god of a man arrived in my life. A man with a calm, capable and kind personality, and with a demeanor that instantaneously brought stability to my recently upturned world. We had similar viewpoints, similar interests, and he just so happened to be a consummate and experienced traveler. Somehow from the depths of my sad soul, I had conjured up just what I needed in my life at that time. My new boyfriend fascinated me with stories of his own adventures, which included biking around six of the seven continents of the world. He not only encouraged me to pursue my dreams, but he gave me the confidence to move forward into my new future. He instilled in me the beliefs that change and growth are healthy and invariably would lead to new doors being opened in my life. He proposed that we head off on a one-year traveling adventure. Not needing any additional prompting I jumped on the opportunity, thrilled that I would not only be fulfilling my aspirations but would also have a seasoned traveler to accompany me on my journey.

I wanted to leave as quickly as possible. I needed to get out of my life before the Grim Reaper knocked on my own door. I quit my beloved veterinary job which now represented good clients, good colleagues and good friends. I sold my vehicle. I gave notice to my landlady. I relocated my geriatric pets to the homes of my friends and family. I withdrew all of my savings and converted them into traveler's checks. I placed all of my possessions into boxes and then I placed all of my boxes into a storage cubicle. I neatly boxed up my current life in preparation for my new one.

We purchased an around-the-world ticket which allowed us to easily move throughout the continents. That year, we traveled by bicycle through Europe, Africa, and Asia camping in each country that we toured. Traveling by bike meant that we were self-sufficient which enabled us financially extend the trip for a much longer period of time than if we had been traveling by bus and from hotel to hotel. It also meant that we would be traveling and living in some extremely remote areas and, hence, would be vulnerable to the hazards of the country that we were traveling through. Food, water poisoning, infectious disease, venomous snakes, hording insects would all become very real possibilities in our daily lives. Since we were traveling in some poverty-stricken countries there was an inherent danger in moving through them, which would necessitate us sticking together as we biked. The trip was everything I wanted: adventure, escape from the sadness of my own life, and fulfillment of my life's bucket list all at the same time. It also, forever after, in only the best of ways, influenced both my personal and professional practices and philosophies.

That year was a trying test of my mental and physical endurance as well as a tremendous test of our relationship. We were at very different levels of athletic ability which inevitably led to frustrations and sometimes intense arguments. For eleven months, twenty four hours a day, and seven days a week, we lived in a tent. Each day we woke up in a cramped canvas home, stiff and sore from the previous day's ride. We cooked our food on a primitive stove. We ate whatever food that we were able to scrounge up from the tiny villages that we passed through on the previous day. A large portion of each day was devoted to finding potable water, and to finding food that had worthwhile energy content. We spent hot, sweaty days biking through dusty and remote terrains. At night we had to search for a safe campsite, and then we had to secretly set up our camps to avoid the crowds of people that gathered around us. If the local villagers got wind of the fact that we were camped nearby, it seemed we would become the evenings theater for the town. They would stand around us in half-circle fashion staring at everything that we did. It also made for nerve wracking nights wondering if anyone from the towns would return to harass us or rob from us. Our life for that year, like a large population of the world, had become about food, water, and safe shelter.

On not too infrequent occasions I was asked to help with a person who was injured or sick. Sometimes they asked because they learned that I was a veterinarian and had medical knowledge, and sometimes they asked because I was a foreigner traveling through a very poor country. It seemed to be a common misnomer of the poverty-stricken people we met that, a) if you were a foreigner you must know something about medicine, and b) that you would have the money or the means to help them. It didn't seem to matter that we were two sweaty, filthy, permanently unemployed bikers who were carrying all of the belongings that we owned in our bicycle saddlebags.

It was sheer luck on their part that I did have some medical knowledge which could be of help to them. Giving medical advice outside of my field was not something that I was typically keen about doing. In the United States giving medical advice without the proper licensing could easily result in a lawsuit, but in developing countries there are often no governing laws to stop you. And the sad reality was that my knowledge and skills actually did exceed what medical help was available to these people who were so isolated in remote areas.

In one tiny village in western Africa we stopped to refresh our water supply. A young man met us at the water pump. His face was swollen and deformed. He gestured at his mouth. I understood from his gestures that he had a tooth abscess and that the infection had spread to the tissue on his face. He could barely open his mouth or speak. The expression in his eyes and his slow lethargic movements reflected the pain that he was living with on a daily basis. Antibiotics and a good dentist, and his problems would have been resolved months ago, but that is not a simple thing for a man living in a remote and destitute village. I gave him three Tylenols, the only pain medication that we were carrying with us on our journey. I prayed that we wouldn't need it ourselves in the immediate future. I knew that it was a somewhat pathetic gesture, but I hoped it would give him some relief from his pain for at least a short time.

One day while traveling on an unshaded dirt road in the hot African savannah my boyfriend complained of feeling weak and dizzy. It was unlike him to complain about anything. We stopped for a rest in the shade of a tree but it soon became obvious that he was very ill and in no condition to bike on. We inquired with a local who gestured that there was a medical clinic within a few miles of us. We were in the far north of a very untraveled country and I was ecstatic when I learned that not only was there a hospital which was relatively close, but there was a German physician working at this hospital.

Having a foreigner treat us, sadly for everyone who didn't have that luxury, could be the difference between life and death for my boyfriend. Foreigners generally had better medical knowledge, better medical skills, better concepts of sterility, and were also more likely to speak English which would improve our ability to communicate my boyfriend's symptoms and understand their recommendations. I knew that as foreigners we would probably receive better care than the locals. There is an unspoken knowledge that if you are a foreigner in Africa you will receive privileges that the locals won't get.

As weak as he was, Ben managed to bike to the hospital. When I say the word hospital, the Western mind conjures up images of tall, windowed, white buildings which are clustered together in a community arrangement. This rural African hospital was a single one-storied building about the size of the post office in the average American town. We walked into a fenced area, wheeling our bikes besides us. The scene before me reminded me of the old war movies that I used to watch on TV. Everywhere, people seemed to be lying on the ground. Some were propped up against the sides of the building and some were sprawled out on the lawn in varying positions of repose. Within the building there was a central courtyard. We again were greeted by the sight of what seemed to be about fifty bodies lying on the ground, some half-conscious, some moaning, some with wraps around their heads or limbs, and some with vomitus or diarrhea surrounding them where they lay.

The hospital rooms were laid out in a circular fashion around the central courtyard. There appeared to be one occupied bed in each room, and one or two people lying on the floors next to the bed. I wondered what criteria of illness, or status level in a village, allowed a person to be placed in a room, or even better, on a bed within a room. There were no IV lines, no pumps, no EKG machines, no charts, and no nurses. Nothing was present that you would normally associate with a hospital. Just what appeared to be a miserable moaning mass of people lying around in the sweltering heat.

After some inquiring, we were directed to the house of the German physician who was in her kitchen eating a quick lunch. She greeted us with surprise. She rarely received foreign visitors in this remote region. She was middle-aged with heavy wrinkles, and tiny – not more than 5'2". She took one look at Ben's pale face and kindly brought him into the guest room of her modest home. She told me that it wouldn't be right to place him amongst the local people at the hospital. It would not be standard or accepted by the locals.

"We must test him for malaria," she said in her staccato accented voice, "and if it is not that, we will treat him for heat stroke."

She started him on an aggressive fluid regimen and placed him in a shaded room with an amply cushioned bed and then drew the appropriate blood samples for testing. I reflected on the fact that because my boyfriend was a foreigner he was lying in a comfortable bed in her home. And he was receiving individual medical care from the region's only physician, while the locals were outside swatting flies off their wounds and waiting for hours, if not days, for care from a poorly trained medic. A foreigner's privilege in action. A privilege which I was guiltily happy to have at that moment.

"I must get back to work," she told me after finishing with him. "There is so much to do. So many ill people. Come out and help if you'd like to," she added after hearing I was a veterinarian.

After assuring myself that Ben was sleeping quietly, I went back to the complex dreading being immersed in so much illness and pain. I followed her around and watched her attend to the various patients, speaking soothingly to them in their native tongue and giving directions to the rare attendee around. She would write orders, change bandages, administer medications, reexamine a patient, receive new patients, chat with their family members and then quickly move on to the next person. She didn't spend much time with any of them but did her best to address their immediate concerns. She did this for hours on end and never seemed to get overwhelmed or distressed by the lack of equipment, lack of basic facilities, or lack of diagnostic capabilities. I helped her as best as I could, changing bandages or holding down protesting limbs, but I felt a little overwhelmed and frustrated with the sheer volume and the severe illnesses of the patients and the lack of proper medical equipment and medications. She told me that she had been working in this facility, in these conditions for over nine years. I was having trouble coping with this environment for nine minutes, never mind nine years. She's Mother Teresa, I thought to myself. An angel, an unsung hero. A person who has selflessly committed herself to taking care of the poor in the harshest of environments and a person who receives little recognition or financial reward for her efforts.

She invited me to join her in a surgical procedure that she was going to perform that evening. The surgery was to be performed on a woman who had a tumor on her uterus that needed to be removed. She told me that it was the first chance she had to do it and, plus, the insects were lower in the evening. This should be interesting, I thought. Hesitating, I nodded my head yes.

The operating room turned out to be an open windowed room, with a few bare cabinets, and a metal table in the middle. The surgery pack was on the table next to the patient who was in the process of being induced with an intravenous anesthetic. I asked what type of anesthetic they were using and I was told it was drip of a drug called Ketamine. No other drugs were being used to anesthetize her. I was appalled once again. Ketamine is an anesthetic which is used in both veterinary medicine and human medicine. It has a dissociative effect. This means that you are in a distant dream-like state and are aware that you are being operated on, you can feel pain, but you cannot move your muscles to do anything about it. In veterinary medicine, it is usually combined with another drug to relieve pain.

The attendant who induced her anesthesia started the Ketamine drip and then left the room. I assumed he was going to return shortly but he never did. The woman remained under general anesthesia, undergoing a major abdominal surgery with nobody observing her to see if her vitals were remaining normal. This anesthetic technique and lack of monitoring seemed to be the routine. Unthinkable, and far below any current medical standard found in veterinary medicine. During the course of the surgery the women kept blurting out sentences in the local African dialect and rolling her head back and forth in seeming protest. Just go to a happy place in your mind, I kept wishing for her as I assisted the German physician. Then I found myself wondering if this patient had any happy vacation places in her memory to refer to.

I watched in amazement as the surgeon-saint made a cut in the woman's abdomen and gently removed the large tumorous uterus from within. The physician had no gown and wore only sterile gloves and a mask. She would intermittently shoo flies away from her incision site. The uterus removal went without complications. The surgeon closed the women up and we transferred her to one of the coveted rooms where she lay uncovered without any monitoring equipment, nurses or postoperative pain medications. She continued to moan and mutter incoherent things to me. I held her hand helplessly with tears streaming down my own face.

She was administered an antibiotic, Chloramphenicol. I was appalled for the thousandth time that day. Chloramphenicol is a very effective antibiotic but a drug that was banned in the United States in humans and in food producing animals due to some of its potentially fatal side effects which admittedly are quite rare.

"It's a good antibiotic," said the physician in a sharp, scolding tone when I expressed my surprise and stated my concern about its side effects, "and it side effects are rare. It is the only one we have, we are grateful to have it."

I was ashamed. If it worked for the majority, then the rare side effect was inconsequential and it beat the alternative of not having any antibiotics at all. I had no right to judge anything that was being done. Just like in the veterinary field, she had to work with she had in front of her, or offer less than optimal treatments than were considered the gold standard of medicine because she had no other options.

Ben recovered uneventfully after several days of rest in the doctor's comfortable home. His malaria tests were negative. We decided retrospectively that he had suffered from heat stroke. We biked off leaving this lady physician to care for the hordes of ill people at her hospital. I wondered what drives a person to continue in those conditions. What drives her to continue to care for people in substandard conditions, with substandard supplies and with inadequate help? How frustrating it must be for her to not be able to effectively help people with very treatable conditions. She's not just Mother Teresa, she's a superhero with supernatural abilities to withstand grief and hardships. People are always questioning my ability to deal with the injuries or deaths of the animals I treat. Compared to this physician, my day is a day in Candy Land. I think of her regularly and wonder where she is. Wherever she is, whether in the depths of some poverty stricken country, or back in her homeland, my hat is off to her.

Arriving in yet another remote village, a resident of the small town approached me to come look at her child. I could see it in her eyes that she was hoping that I was the savior who had arrived to help her and her child. I thought I was immune to disease and hardship by now but what she brought me to see in her thatched-roof dirt hut stunned and overwhelmed me. The first image I have of her child sticks in my mind like a well-worn photograph. This child's images will periodically flash in my memory when I am counseling the owners of one of my veterinary patients. Lying under a thin, dirty cloth was an emaciated, dehydrated waif of a figure. All skin and bones, she appeared to be a living skeleton rather than a child. She was curled up in the fetal position on a grass mat on the dirt floor. Large sunken eyes peered up at me silently when I approached. She was too sick to move or to respond to me.

"What's wrong with her?" I asked. Through gestures and partial interpretations they explained she was a diabetic.

"Does she have insulin?" I asked, knowing the answer before I asked.

This family was barely subsisting. They made their wages from selling the rare fruit from a spindly, diseased looking tree that grew in the front of their yard. They didn't have money for their own meals or for daily living, never mind the money to purchase insulin and manage a diabetic child. There was no electricity in this town or even a water well for that matter. They were drinking water directly from the filthy river that ran behind the town.

The extended family went about their daily routines stepping over the child with the casualness that they would walk over a piece of furniture which was in their way. They continued grinding their corn, and scrubbing their laundry, and cooking their meals over the open fire as if nothing was unusual. Their level of complacency and acceptance was what really struck me. It's not that they didn't know that she was dying, and it was not that they didn't care about her. It was that within their lives and their means there was nothing they could do about it but to accept her fate. It was part of life in their remote little village.

The family had brought me, an unheard-of Westerner, into their home to see her in the hopes that my knowledge and advice could help her. The truth was that I was as helpless as they were in this matter. My first instinct was to grab her and rush her to the nearest hospital, which was a mere two hundred miles away over a dusty, bumpy road in an overcrowded bus. And then the practicalities of the situation sunk in. Even if I did get her to a city alive and funded her initial medical care, then who was going to continue her care afterwards. The twice-daily insulin injections, the constant rechecks, and the intermittent hospitalizations she would need would be impossible for this family. She's dying, I thought to myself, there is nothing I can do. Just like her family I needed to accept her fate.

Fast-forward to ten years later, I am working as an emergency veterinarian in the United States and I am standing over a dog who has been placed on a ventilator because he is no longer capable of breathing on his own. A ventilator is a sophisticated and expensive machine which will breathe for a person or an animal and will allow them to stay alive until they can resume their own spontaneous breathing. If they are going to resume spontaneous breathing is always the big question when an animal is placed on a ventilator. The dog is elderly – maybe twelve years of age. X-rays had revealed that he has a large tumor which is taking up one entire lung field. The owners elect to ventilate him in the hopes that we could stabilize him until surgery. Full ventilation costs about

$3000 for a twenty-four-hour period. If he undergoes surgery, the bill may triple. If the dog has lung cancer then his lifespan at best will be six months to a year after surgery. The costs or his prognosis didn't seem to faze his owners who wanted to do anything to keep him alive, even if it was only for a few more hours.

This is ridiculous, I thought while I monitored the dog who, I was fairly certain, would never leave our hospital. All of this money, just to keep a dog alive for a few hours or a few more months. I reflected back to the little girl and her family in western Africa. I was sure she was long ago dead from her diabetes. I wondered what her family would think of the fact that I was here ventilating a dog, with a terminal disease, for an exorbitant sum of money. Money which would have easily kept their child alive until she was old and grey. My emotions were mixed. Shame for the world as a whole being unable to help children like her, mixed with the understanding that the wealth of the world has always been divided unfairly. This couple has every right to treat their dog exactly as they want to with their own money.

It is not unusual for people to come into our ER hospital with an injured pet and quickly realize that they are unable to care for it because the treatment is financially beyond their means. Sometimes they are angry and other times they are apologetic. A long explanation follows which reflects the torment that they are feeling over having to make a decision which is based on their finances. They are guilt-ridden that they have to place a price on their beloved animal's life.

"There is no need to apologize, I understand completely." My response is sincere. I have a very real understanding of why they are making that decision.

Just like that family in Africa who had accepted that they could not help their dying diabetic child, and just like the many millions of people in the world who need to accept similar fates for their families, these people would need to accept that they would not be able to care for their pet within the means or the circumstances of their own lives. Sometimes, if it seems appropriate, I share my travel stories with them. I want them to hear about how other people live and to use these stories to put things into perspective.

I am sad for all of these people and I am sad for their pets. I am sad when people who are in financially bad situations arrive and can't afford the treatment. I am sad when parents with injured pets arrive who are struggling just to feed their families and to pay their rent. I am sad when a budget-restricted elderly person arrives with an ailing elderly pet that they have nurtured their whole lives.

To help me cope with these heartbreaking daily scenarios I remind myself of the even more heartbreaking scenarios that I was immersed in while traveling through poverty-stricken cultures. I compare the situation in front of me to what is happening on a more global perspective. It is the only way I can survive my job. Every time there is a sad outcome because people can't afford the extensive medical care that their animal might need, I remind myself that these are the injustices of the world, and that these injustices are affecting millions of people in this world. They are far more wide-spread and harsh than what I have to deal with within the walls of my hospital. They have existed for centuries. And that is why some people live in refugee camps in metal shacks using newspaper as insulation, while other people have second and third vacation homes. And that is why there are potbellied, malnutritioned children and adults in the world while the majority of American dogs and cats are obese. And that is why some people can ventilate their dying dog, while elsewhere children in destitute countries die from diabetes.

Money and access to medical care are real factors which have, and always will drive the decisions and medical outcomes of a sick person or a sick animal. I cope with the needless euthanasias and the less than ideal medical choices that I may have to perform during my veterinary shifts by remembering that there is a whole harsh world out there and that this dying or injured animal is just one tiny injustice in the universe's grand scheme.

CHAPTER 12

CAMELS, BABOONS, AND MAMBAS

Traveling by bike during our year's journey meant that we had no physical home to live in. The reality of that was that we had no true shelter from inclement weather and zero privacy from the people that we encountered. The realities of being a cycle tourist meant that I now found myself shivering under bridges for protection from the rain, sitting in ditches to cool off at lunch break, and huddling behind rocks for shelter on windy days. I learned with a harsh, unmistakable clarity what life was really like when a person was truly without a home. Included in our concerns was the dangerous wildlife that we might encounter in each of the countries that we traveled through. And though we did encounter an amazing assortment of wildlife while cycle-touring through the continents, as a rule, the mammals that we had to be the most wary of were of the species called Homo sapiens.

While traveling when we biked into a village to resupply ourselves, particularly in the more poverty stricken countries, the townspeople would follow us around in large groups and swarm around us when we stopped. If we went into the market for supplies or went to gather water, one of us would always have to stand close to the loaded bikes to ward off any errant hands. The crowds would work in teams, one person would attempt to distract us while another person from the crowd would reach into our saddle bags to grab our belongings. Each of the items that we carried in our bike bags was vitally important to our daily survival and we guarded our limited possessions fiercely. Losing a cable from our stove would mean we had no way to cook our food, losing a tire pump would leave us stranded in uncertain areas if we got a flat tire, and losing a sleeping bag would mean very cold nights shivering under a cheaply constructed blanket that we had to purchase at a local market.

In the evenings when we stopped to set up camp, we would search to find a camping spot that was hidden from sight of the locals. Usually this meant camping within the woods or the jungle terrain. Hiding our camp was an attempt to avoid the throngs of locals who, if they discovered our site, would invariably gather around our tent and spend their evening staring at us. When this happened we had the impression that we were the town's evening entertainment as a crowd of people sitting in a semi-circle just a few feet away from our tents, would watch as we set up our gear and our tent. When we went looking for bathroom privacy they would follow us to watch.

Even though we only had a few belongings and minimum clothing, it still seemed that we had far more than the locals did. We were in a mosquito-proof tent, while they were swatting at the clouds of biting insects which were swarming through their huts. We had aluminum tent poles that snapped together quickly to form a shelter while they had spindly huts created from poor quality wood. We had a fuel-powered camping stove, while they had to gather firewood often at far distances from their villages. We had a water filter, they drank contaminated river water. We had pasta which was a coveted luxury, while they were eating nutrition less rice that would often have teeth-cracking rocks mixed in with its grains. In bad weather, we remained dry in our waterproof tent, while they became drenched as water leaked through their mud sealed thatched roofs. By our own country's standards the minimum belongings that we owned at that time made us destitute, but in comparison to the people of these villages we were wealthy.

As a veterinarian and a traveler, I couldn't help but notice the medical infractions and substandard care of the animals we observed. Typically in the poorest of countries, the livestock are treated quite well while the non-food providers, like dogs and cats, are left to fend for themselves with little compassion or care. One country in particular, Morocco, stood out as having some of the worst treatment of the animals of burden that I saw in our travels that year. At the time that we were traveling, donkeys were an abundant and important mode of transport in this country. Yet the donkeys all seemed overloaded with giant sacks of firewood or grain. These heavy loads were placed on top of primitive wooden saddles that would create festering sores on the donkeys' backs. The most offensive infraction to me was that these animals had hand-made wire bits which created large painful ulcers in their mouths. The donkeys were dragged around the narrow city streets by these sharp thin bits, with the men flogging them mercilessly if they didn't move fast enough.

I was equally as horrified when I witnessed a group of men binding the feet of a loudly braying ewe and then shoving the protesting beast into the trunk of their tiny car. Once she was situated in the trunk, they slammed the hood down and proceeded off to market where she would be sold. The locals of this country seemed to not care an inch about the welfare of the animals that were providing an important means to their existence

Now snakes are one of my least favorite creatures in the world, but I was still aghast to see that the snake charmers, who were so popular in the Moroccan tourist markets, sewed the mouths of the cobras shut. This surgery was performed as a safety precaution to prevent the snakes from biting the snake handlers and the onlookers, but it also prevented the hapless reptiles from eating. This didn't seem to matter to the handlers who depended on these tourist-attracting creatures for their mode of existence. I was once again disgusted when I saw a street hustler pulling two snakes from a bucket of cold water which was sitting next to him. The large snakes lay on the ground flaccid and immobile from the cold water in which they had been immersed. Except for their size, there was nothing terribly impressive about these two supposedly venomous snakes. *Not such brave snake handlers after all* I thought to myself. I was angry enough about the treatment of animals in this country to report my observations to an international watch group, but I had little hope that anything would change.

I was pleasantly surprised to find that the people in China treated their pets and livestock with more respect than I had anticipated. I had seen several documentaries showing horrific acts of violence against animals in this country, yet the stray dogs in the areas that we traveled through seemed well fed and were not warily skulking around in anticipation of flying stones. I was equally impressed when a farmer in a small Himalayan town, upon learning the nature of my profession, asked me to evaluate an abscess that had formed on the skin beneath his donkey's tail strap. His concern was that the wound was causing his donkey discomfort while it was carrying its pack. While treating the abscess, a small crowd of local villagers stood around watching me work. I recognized the odd humor about the fact that I was treating an abscess on a burro's butt, while standing in the heart of the Himalayan Mountains in geography that had used to be called Tibet. I was not far from the town about which it is believed the book titled *Shangri La* had been written. Here I was living the dream of a veterinarian. I was practicing medicine in my own personal Shangri La. So what if my medical task just happened to be focused on the ass of a donkey.

As bike tourists, we were often harassed by the people of the towns that we biked through. They were used to tourists who drove rapidly through their towns in air-conditioned, dark windowed SUV's. We were on bikes, not fast moving vehicles, which made us fair game for their tormenting. It seemed that the children and teenagers of each town had little to do but harass us. They would follow us for miles, peddling their single-gear, broken-down bikes that didn't have brakes or proper handles, weaving in and out of our heavily-laden bikes just for the sheer fun of it. Sometimes they would band up in large frenzied groups and throw rocks at us as we passed by, or try to stick sugar cane into our spokes in the hopes of creating a yard sale of items that they could run off with when we went down. In Africa it was a common practice to throw rocks at the stray dogs and cats. Apparently as "poor" white people, unable to afford air-conditioned tour vehicles, we were in the same category as the stray animals who roamed their cities.

One sweltering day in northwestern Africa, I become progressively angrier at the groups of children who were freely whizzing rocks at me. I stopped, got off my bike, and yelled at a group of mothers who were standing passively around watching their children fling rocks at us with vicious intent.

"Your children are throwing rocks at us, do something about it," I yelled at the women.

I was pantomiming the children's actions to the parents so they would understand what my words and my tone meant. The group of ladies were startled enough by this sweaty, dirt-smeared, overly animated white woman screaming at them, to be goaded into action. One of the women responded by bending down, picking up a large rock and tossing it with vigor and amazing accuracy at the children who were throwing rocks at us. The children scattered as soon as the woman bent over, realizing instantly what was about to come. *Never mind*, I decided biking away. I was wasting my time. Now I had a better understanding of why their children behaved in this way.

My travels have given me unusual opportunities to experience the variety of animal transportation modalities. In Thailand, I traveled for three days by elephant through a thick jungle. I was a bit scared of the beasts as there were stories of them becoming unexpectedly violent. They were wild animals after all, and this was definitely not an arena of Ringling Brothers. I was petrified when the creature wrapped its trunk around me to place me onto its head. Suddenly, I found myself eye to very-large-eye with a giant beast whose scratchy, wiry hair was rubbing abrasively against me. Somehow my foot seemed to find a holding spot in its enormous mouth... not exactly the placement that I wanted. Gripped in the wraps of this powerful beast I was reminded of how miniscule I was in the grand scheme of things. Instead of hurting me, the elephant gently and carefully placed me on top of its head. I sat on the saddle, awed as it nimbly carried us through rough and steep terrain in the Thai jungle. Their dexterity is astonishing, considering their cumbersome size.

In the Sahara desert I rode another bizarre and fascinating beast of burden – a camel – through the dunes for a day. After riding horses all of my life, I was astonished by how weak and floppy these creatures' necks are and that their necks can be controlled by a thin rein attached to a ring in the nose. With my pinky finger, I could effortlessly pull the camel's nose around to my knee, as it seemed to have no muscled strength in its neck to resist. I tried sitting in all of the possible positions you can sit in while on a camel's back. I learned that the back-hump seat is the Cadillac of spots when riding a camel and is far more comfortable than the front-hump seat. I laughed in glee as the thing awkwardly loped its way around the desert's dunes. I experienced a true desert for the first time and it has become one of the most stunningly beautiful places I have ever seen. I learned how sensuous and mystical dunes can be as they change from gold to orange to red depending on the light. And how the sand of the dunes flows around you, almost like a river, as you walk over them. I stayed far away from the ornery camels at night. I had been warned earlier by the Berber tribespeople that the camels were likely to spit or kick out if you approached too close. They would hunker down in a butts-to-the-exterior circle as protection from the wind. Knowing full well the power of horses, I had a healthy respect for large beasts and kept at a safe distance from them. I noticed, though, that their feet had swollen mushroom like soles that appeared to be much softer than horses feet looked.

In northern India we encountered the Yaks while hiking into the mountains of the Himalayan range. There, most of the tourists rented Yaks to carry their packs up the mountains. My rugged and semi-masochistic boyfriend insisted that we carry our own. Travelers warned us to always step back toward the mountain side of the trails when the nervous half-wild Yaks passed by us in order to avoid being pushed off of the steep cliffs. Every year tourists were killed by the harmless enough appearing beasts in what we came to refer as "Yak attacks." In one frightening moment, we were pinned against a wall by a maternal Yak as she passed us on the narrow trail. She apparently did not like the odd and unusual appearance of people carrying their own luggage on their backs. I used that as yet another argument to my stubborn boyfriend for why we should not be carrying our own backpacks.

We also had plenty of odd experiences with the wild animals of the countries that we traveled through. In Cameroon, we biked thirty miles along a deserted dirt road into a game park filled with wild elephants, hippos, crocs, and lions. It probably is not as dangerous as one would imagine, as the animals are hard to find and the territory is vast, but it was probably not as safe as we were trying to make it out to be either. When we arrived at our destination, which was a small group of huts in the center of the game park, we set up our tent on the outskirts of the village. Within a few hours a family of baboons sauntered by with the largest female carrying a baby on her back. Baboons in Africa are a bit like raccoons in America. They are pesky creatures who raid the garbage, leave feces in inappropriate places, and steal objects and food from the huts. When angered, they bare their lips and expose large glossy white fangs, a sight frightening and intimidating enough to back most people off. We were entranced by a mother baboon who kept wandering close enough for us to get adorable photo-ops of her and her baby which was piggybacked on top of her. I turned around in the middle of her photo session to find the male baboon emerging from our tent with a bag filled with our food bag in his mouth. I quickly understood that the mama baboon had purposefully lured us away from the tent. Now we had just biked a long way along rutted, insect infested, dirt roads to get to the game park and there was a limited quantity of food that we could carry on the bike. Our food was precious and necessary for us to be able to bike out of the park. We were a long, difficult day away from a town, and our only food was being carried off in the fangs of a large and aggressive male baboon.

I was mad enough that I tried to follow him into the brush and scare the big male into dropping the bag, but he hissed and spit and stamped at me with enough drama to frighten me. He then went off into the bushes with his family. Angrily I watched from a respectful distance as he tore into our food bag and explored the contents. The family of baboons spent the next several hours in the bushes, peering out at us, and waiting for the opportune moment to raid our tent again. We were at war, but this time we would not be fooled and we stood vigilantly guarding our possessions. Like a bad scene from the movie, *The Planet of the Apes*, we valiantly defended our territory. We gathered rocks and placed them as piles of ammunition in front of us, intermittently flinging them at the group to keep them at bay. We gathered sticks to use in case they came too close. Luckily for us, the local game park residents took pity on us and supplied us with food to use during our departure trip, only at a much higher cost than we would have spent had we been purchasing food in the villages. The locals were no fools. They were good entrepreneurs, understanding that they had no competition.

We had quite a few harrowing experiences that year that I wish I could forget. Snakes are rampant in this part of Africa and we were warned that all of the snakes in this region were toxic. If we saw one, we were cautioned to stay far away from it. Cobras, vipers, and mambas were some of the deadliest. The insidious presence of snakes was evident by the large number of dead bodies that we saw littered over the roads as we biked through this relatively unpopulated country. There were horrifically long snakes, fat snakes, colorful snakes, skinny snakes, flat snakes, smooth snakes, and rough snakes. Dead snakes of every size and shape reminded us of the live ones that must be present in the brush where we had to camp. I was terrified of stepping on one, or finding one curled up next to our tents in the morning seeking the heat of the occupied tent.

One day I biked up to my boyfriend who was perpetually ahead of me, and who was usually waiting for me, frustrated and impatient. This time, I found him sitting on the bank of a shallow ditch calmly eating his lunch. To the left of him, almost within petting distance, a large brown cobra lay curled up calmly surveying him as if they were old, casual friends.

"SSSSSnaaake," I hissed pointing at the ground just to the left of him.

My presence seemed to rouse the thing and it slithered off, not nearly as excited about the encounter as I was.

"Where?" said Ben, continuing to chew his mouthful of food and looking obliviously around him. Despite both of us being exhausted, I insisted that we move on from that spot as I had visions of stalking cobras dancing through my head.

One day after biking for a long ways through an open, baking savannah terrain, we arrived at a beautiful and dreamlike forest of ancient teak trees. Teak trees are majestic trees and their thick canopy of leaves provide a lovely shaded respite from the powerful sun. We biked in tandem through the shaded corridor, grateful for the quiet and cool calmness that the forest offered. The dirt road was littered with large spade-shaped leaves which formed a green blanket under our tires. I biked over one large leaf in the center of the road and without warning, a thin, green snake maybe five or six feet in length reared up from beneath the leaf and paused for just the briefest of moments with his pointed face just at the height of my thigh. Although my imagination and storytelling prowess would like to say that it reared up towards me, in actuality I think it was trying as hard to get away from me as I was trying to get away from it. I leaned my body and my bike down and to the left, as it tilted its head and body away from me to the right. It then turned and rapidly slid away at a sharp angle from my bike, pulling its tail out from the edge of my wheel as it moved off. My boyfriend stopped abruptly to avoid biking over it as well. The encounter left us both gasping and frozen with fear. There is only one bright green snake in Cameroon...the green mamba, a snake which is considered one of the deadliest in the world. The leaves in front of us suddenly become land mines as we weren't sure which one in the long path ahead of us was also hiding a venomous viper beneath it. I had just biked over a green mamba and I had lived to tell the tale.

Luckily, other experiences with the beasts of the world were more positive, sometimes even magical. Rounding a curve of the road, we came across a herd of giraffes that were lounging nearby. My heart was in my throat looking at these beautiful, yet awkward creatures. Startled by our presence, the giraffes bounded off at a dead run. It was the way that they ran which struck me the most. They had this strange, slow loping gait which see-sawed from nose to tail in a perpetual rhythm. In a close group they ran together with their heads and long necks moving in graceful unison through the low trees of the savannah. As I watched, the sounds of an orchestra reverberated loudly in my mind. They rocked and flowed, and rocked and flowed in continuity across the field. I felt lucky to be standing somewhere in a remote part of western Africa. I felt sorry for every other human being on earth who was not there to witness the amazing sight I was seeing. I had never seen a group of animals so cohesive and so poetic. Although I am not a religious person in the traditional sense, I knew that the loud symphony which was playing into my ears as they ran in unison, could only have been emitting from the loudspeakers of Heaven.

CHAPTER 13

I AM AN ER VETERINARIAN

The average career of a veterinarian who works emergency shifts is about six years. This is because the job has a multitude of responsibilities and stressors, both physical and mental that take fortitude, persistence, steel will and physical stamina. If you lack any of those traits, or lose them along the way, then it is prudent to get out of the job before it kills you. I can say that with the voice of experience because practicing emergency medicine almost did kill me.

Working as an emergency doctor is a different ballgame from working as a family veterinarian. As an emergency vet you are meeting people for the first time and it is usually under stressful circumstances. Your clients arrive at your hospital in the wee hours of the night, anxious, upset and frightened for their pet whose condition has just taken a dramatic turn for the worse. These people don't know you, they don't trust you, and you are now working on a member of their family who is in a crisis situation.

"It takes a certain personality to do ER medicine," a friend of mine who is a family veterinarian told me. "That kind of person needs to enjoy the chaos, the excitement, the unpredictability, the lack of a schedule, and the lack of long term relationships with their clients." She paused thoughtfully and added, "I enjoy being a family vet. Give me my routine appointments and my healthy pet checkups. That's what makes me happy. ER work is not for everybody."

She was right. Emergency medicine is not for everybody. Chaos, excitement, unpredictability, and the complete lack of any routine schedule. Sign me up because I have no interest in ever having to see a lineup of vaccinations and ear infections on a fixed schedule again.

"That's what you always wanted to do," my first boss reminded me after I returned from our year long around-the-world trip, where interestingly enough excitement, unpredictability and lack of any semblance of a routine schedule had also been my life, and I told him that I had taken a job as an emergency veterinarian. I had forgotten that I had expressed that desire so early on in my career. Truly, the specialized field of emergency veterinary medicine must be my calling.

Typically the shifts that emergency veterinarians work are overnights, weekends, and holidays. These are the shifts when the day practices are not open and in which family veterinarians no longer want to work. It was not until the emergence of 24-hour veterinary hospitals or the development of cooperative systems of on -call shifts between the hospitals in a particular region that family veterinarians finally got the well-deserved respite that they needed. Respite from being on- call throughout the weekends and from being called in for an emergency during the evening after they had already worked overtime that same day. It does not take long for burnout to set in when you are at the perpetual demand of your clients, particularly when the majority of emergencies are really only emergencies in the eyes of the client.

It's not the emergency work but the night shifts that almost killed me. Night shifts are an entity of their own. Ask anyone, in any field, who has done night shifts and you will learn how wearing these hours are on your body and on your mind. A ten hour day shift is really not equivalent either mentally or physically to a ten hour night shift. The fatigue factor seems to triple when working overnights and even on your days off it seems impossible to shake the sense of exhaustion that envelops you. When working consecutive nightshifts my muscles are taut and aching and my body's normal regulatory systems seem to malfunction. The ability to regulate my body temperature is the most consistent system to go haywire. When three in the morning rolls around, even on a hot summer night, I invariably find myself shivering and snuggled up to a space heater, wrapped in blankets. By mid-evening my eyes would become dry and blurred. It was not until I started night shifts that I was forced to trade my contact lenses for my glasses due to the inability to focus my parched eyes. Clearly the cells in my body which were responsible for lubricating my eyes were fast asleep at three in the morning and they seemed to be loudly telling my body to join them in bed where it belonged. The portion of my brain which is designed to mitigate my emotions also seemed to be napping as justifiably it should be. Without fail, mid-evening my emotions would start to fire out of control. Outbursts of sadness, anger, helplessness, or fear would envelop me without warning. It was not unusual for me to become overwhelmed with feelings of sadness or intense anxiety in the middle of the night, or in the morning to drive home with tears rolling down my face for reasons that I could never rationally explain.

One early morning I was on the phone with a client when I fell fast asleep with the hand piece still pressed to my ear. I woke up a minute later realizing that I had slept through her question. I slapped my face and asked her to repeat herself struggling not to fall asleep a second time as she repeated the question. This is ridiculous I would tell myself each morning when my shift was over, this is not healthy, I need to get myself off of night shifts. I need to find a job that only works the hours when the sun is still out, but then out of love for the job and because of distasteful memories of treating routine ear infections and anal gland infections I would persevere the next shift, forgetting how bad things could be until I was once again immersed in the chaos of the moment.

In my particular job I work in a specialty and referral veterinary hospital. A specialty hospital is staffed with a group of veterinarians who have been board certified in a particular area of veterinary medicine. Areas of specialty are similar to those seen in human medicine and include such fields as veterinary oncology ophthalmology, surgery, internal medicine, radiologists and dermatologists. Veterinarians who have become certified in these areas have spent an additional four years in a residency training which then allows them to work as certified specialists in their field. Referral and specialty veterinary hospitals contain a group of boarded specialists who are experts in their particular field and who work together to treat an animal. In the past twenty years the number of these specialty and referral veterinary hospitals has increased exponentially and almost every major city in America has at least one.

At my hospital where we have three board certified surgeons every animal that arrives through the emergency department and who needs surgery is transferred to the care of one of these surgeons. As an emergency veterinarian working in this type of hospital, this translates into having to call a sleepy and usually irritated surgeon late in the evening, to come in and perform surgery on a dog who needs immediate surgery. You first need to have the courage to wake up a cranky, tired surgeon and then justify to that surgeon first, why you need him to come in at that moment in time and then why you are calling him in at 2:00 a.m. when the dog arrived to the hospital at 10:00 in the evening. Although there are usually very valid reasons for the delay of my phone call, such as it took that long for the staff to get the owners to sign the consent form, or that my initial diagnostics weren't conclusive enough to call in the surgeon at an earlier time, or that I had to take care of the arriving hordes of clients and their pets before I could attend to the dog that needed surgery, the surgeon's reactions to my mid-evening phone calls were often quite dramatic. Dramatic enough, at least in the beginning years of my employment there, that I had to mentally steel myself for their response before I picked up the phone receiver to call them in. My suspicions were that the surgeons believed that the ER staff was intentionally plotting against them, and that we maliciously and purposefully delayed the surgery time until the middle of the night just to irritate them as well as to insure the ruin of the harmony of the following day for them.

The truth is that I am no happier than the surgeons that they have to drive into the hospital at some crazy hour of the night to perform a surgery on my shift. Their angry demeanor and actions would upset me and my night staff. Just come in here and do your job, is what I wanted to say to them and stop screaming at me for doing my job. I refrained from speaking these words because I realize that at that time of night and at this point in the shift, I probably was not acting rationally either and it was not going to make the situation any more pleasant. Over time when a mutual respect was firmly established between both teams their behaviors thankfully became tempered.

By the end of my overnight shift at my specialty hospital, I have to have the stamina and backbone to walk into morning rounds to transfer the information about the patients that I treated overnight to the daytime veterinary specialists. Typically I am exhausted from a stressful night, full of a myriad of emotions and action packed events that no one but myself knows about or cares about. You then have to prove to these doctors that you cared for the in-hospital patients with skill and with care. And when all of your cases are wrapped up, and you have communicated with the clients, communicated with the family veterinarians, written all the discharge instructions, written all of the records, survived morning rounds, transferred your cases to the specialists and updated your technicians about your patients, then and only then then do you get to go home to sleep and be ready to return bright eyed and sharp in six to eight hours. At least in my early days as an ER veterinarian, before we had additional help from veterinary interns, it was not unusual for an overnight shift to have lasted between fourteen and sixteen hours and for us to have done four or more of these shifts consecutively.

Night shifts have the tendency to make the people who work them feel isolated and withdrawn from the world. The fact that emergency veterinarians work alone and rarely overlap with our colleagues contributes to these feelings of isolation. We are awake when our friends and family are not, we miss most evening and weekend gatherings, and we work most holidays. It is a proven fact that people who work nights are more likely to suffer from depression, substance abuse, general illness and even cancer. In my years working as an ER vet, I saw one emergency veterinarian leave veterinary medicine from intestinal ulcers, another developed chronic intractable diarrhea, still another developed symptoms of psychoses, two veterinarians needed to be placed on antidepressants, and one emergency veterinarian developed colon cancer that reoccurred after nearly fifteen years of being cancer free. Colon cancer is the one type of cancer which has specifically been associated with working nightshifts. I also saw numerous technicians fold from the fatigue and severe depression that began to affect them as a result of working the overnights.

For the early years at our veterinary hospital we had a bedroom. The bed was an old cot with springs that would poke into your sides and if you attempted to sleep on it you would wake up stiffer and sorer then when you first lay down. The sheets were nasty and stained, and seemed to be changed infrequently. There was a fat hospital cat who would visit the room and who we once caught spraying urine on top of the only pillow in there. Initially the overnight ER doctors were all men, and someone had inappropriately hung large posters of Daisy Duke and Pamela Anderson on the walls of the small room, making me wonder what the men doctors were doing in there on their downtime. I countered their posters with photos of young, muscular construction men but all of the images were quickly taken down by someone who did not appreciate the décor.

Sleeping is only allowed if all of your patients are stable and your records are done. It was unacceptable to sleep if there was a critical patient in the hospital, or to not get up to check on a patient's status, or to refuse to speak to an owner when they phoned and asked for you even if it was twilight hours. One young vet rightfully lost his job when he repeatedly went to bed early each night without properly caring for his patients. The last straw came when he left a technician alone to deal with a cat that was gasping and struggling to breathe while he went off to take a nap.

Sometimes at three in the morning on a slow shift the hospital workers would get punch silly. One of our emergency doctors, who was a sideline cowboy, showed the technicians how to rope the rolling ER gurney like he would a steer. One night, in the process of being roped, the uncooperative gurney tipped over and its metal corner punched a hole in the wall. The managers never understood why the gurney would no longer mechanically rise and fall like it used to do. Everyone would just shrug their shoulders with a grin when asked about it. On other nights, this same broad-bodied cowboy would dim all the overhead lights, stand on the treatment table under the bright beam of the surgery light and dance disco for the room. He found his five minutes of fame under the surgery lights on a veterinary exam room table surrounded by clapping technicians. His silly antics would get us all laughing unstoppably and provided a much needed release from the stresses of the night. Other nights we would make a conscious effort to gather as a group in an effort to change the negative momentum of the night. We would practice a few soulful minutes of yoga, or draw colorful pictures as art therapy, or cut vetwrap tape into colorful figurines that we could stick onto the bandages of our surgical patients. These much needed mental breaks would allow us to change the group's energy and allow us to return to our sick patients in a more peaceful and gentle state of mind.

In the morning after an overnight, I needed the mental strength to drive home safely. I would struggle to focus, sometimes driving on autopilot unsure of the driving decisions that I had made when I finally did arrive. Upon entering my house, at the end of my work shift, I occasionally popped open a beer to help me unwind and to help me get to sleep faster. I can only hope that my neighbors would understand why I was sipping a beer on my porch at nine in the morning.

I was not immune to the illnesses and adverse effects that nightshift work brings on. Sleep started to become a problem for me. When I returned home, my mind would continue to whirl with the cases and the clients that I had seen the night before and my body seemed to be physically buzzing despite my best efforts to wind down. I would try to force myself to sleep for the six hours that I had allotted to me, but when it is bright sunlight outdoors, sleep becomes difficult to effectively achieve. Compounding the issue was the fact that our shifts would often switch from weekend days to weekday nights often multiple times within the same month. Eventually my body lost track of when it was supposed to sleep. I couldn't sleep in the hours between my shifts, then I couldn't sleep on the consecutive days off in between the shifts and then I just wasn't sleeping at all.

After seven years of working nights, with the constant stresses, lack of a normal sleeping pattern, isolation from families and friends, and a constant state of fatigue that I just couldn't shake, I became severely depressed myself. The best way I have heard depression described is as if you have been affected with walking pneumonia, only it is walking depression. It is a fever that you have all day long, all of the time, and that you just cannot shake. There is a two foot wide cloud that surrounds your body and physically and psychologically separates you from every person with whom you interact. You feel dead inside and you just can't recover.

"My soul, my vibrant being was nowhere to be found." quoted one talented actress.

I love that statement because it so artfully describes exactly how I felt. My depression became so bad that I was having trouble just physically functioning through simple tasks. My mind felt cloudy, I couldn't focus on the tasks I was performing, I couldn't think through basic problems, and eventually my physical health became affected, even my hands began to tremor when I worked. I finally took an extended time off from doing night shifts and my employer was kind enough to allow me to continue on the weekend day shifts, but I still couldn't shake the unending feelings of gloom and fatigue. Mentally and physically exhausted from this debilitating disease that I just could not get a handle on or shake off, I consulted a physician who placed me on an antidepressant. The medication acted almost immediately. After all of that agonizing and black fuzzy period, the simple act of ingesting a pill resulted in the dark fog dissipating from around my body. I suddenly felt like a human being who wanted to interact with the world again. My vibrant soul had finally returned back into my body and indeed, it was a joyous feeling.

"You must have just been completely serotonin deprived," my surprised physician told me after learning how quickly I responded to the medication. "It usually takes several weeks to see a response."

I felt mad at myself that it had taken me so long to seek help when I was so overwhelmed by this debilitating disease. The fact that a pill that corrected a hormonal balance worked so rapidly reinforced my understanding that depression is truly a disease just like people with low thyroid levels improve when they are supplemented with the hormone thyroxine. Unfortunately it is usually not a disease that other people in your life recognize or want to understand. I felt foolish that I was prescribing medications to help the diseases of a family's pet but I had been terrified to seek help or to try a well described and often effective treatment myself. I felt sad for people who could not overcome this overwhelming disease even with the addition of medication.

I learned a lot from my struggles with depression. I learned that people who have a lot of strengths will mask what is going on until they become so severely depressed that they are not functioning. I learned that I was in the company of such brilliant, creative and successful people as Emily Dickinson, Betty Ford, Ellen DeGeneres, Monica Seles, Chevy Chase, Winston Churchill, Jim Carrey, Robin Williams, Vincent Van Gogh, and Mike Wallace. This disease, and their recovery from it, had served to drive them all towards greatness. I also learned that by speaking openly about depression, you can give hope and strength to other people who feel hopelessly stuck in the middle of it.

"I don't know how you do it," is another common comment that I hear quite frequently from friends and family who are aware that I work the nightshifts.

And the truth is that sometimes I don't know how I do it either. On the days when it seems that I cannot do this even one minute more I mentally refer back to the year that we traveled by bike and how overwhelming and exhausting and impossible it had seemed to be. I had never been an athletic person, had never played on a sports team, had never before been on a bike ride that exceeded twenty miles, had never been forced to survive simply relying on only the few objects that I was carrying with me, and yet I had persevered through its challenges and I had accomplished the route that we had set out to do. It was a physical and mental challenge that had been nothing short of daunting, even to the most adventurous or athletic or self-sufficient of people. And it is that knowledge, and the memory of what I had accomplished and achieved that year, which gave me the courage and strength to continue on through each overwhelmingly stressful and emotional emergency shift. It was because I knew that the challenges that I faced as an ER veterinarian did not even begin to hold a candle to the difficulties that I had persevered through during our year like touring.

But ultimately, what truly keeps me going in this line of work, is that I truly enjoy what I do. I enjoy helping an ill pet through its disease and I enjoy using my skill and knowledge and resources to help people whose pet needs medical attention. It is this one factor, that of true personal satisfaction with the vocation that I have chosen, which has enabled me to continue doing it through all of these years. And it is that one thing which I would advise to anyone who is seeking out a future career. Above all else, make sure that whatever road you choose to walk, that it be in a field that you truly enjoy because there are few other incentives that will keep you content and on track in the long arduous journey that we all have to undertake in life.

CHAPTER 14

THESE ARE A FEW OF
MY FAVORITE THINGS

The last time I went into a human emergency room there was a sign on the wall which read :

AN EMERGENCY BASED ON A LACK OF PLANNING ON YOUR PART
DOES NOT CONSTITUTE AN EMERGENCY ON OUR PART.

I laughed as I knew exactly what they meant. All too often people show up to our hospital with a minor medical problem in their pet and expect that, since this an emergency hospital, they will be seen with the priority of a critical emergency. We do our best, but emergency hospitals do not work on an appointment basis. If numerous owners show up at once, there is bound to be a long wait and the pets with the most serious medical problems will be treated first. This is a system called triaging. Animals are evaluated when they first arrive and the sickest of animals are given priority care.

The majority of patients that arrive don't truly have emergencies. We see a large number of non- life-threatening conditions such as lacerations, abscesses, back pain, urinary tract infections, and broken nails.

About five percent of the cases we see are true, *you may die if we don't intervene,* emergencies. The rest are there because the animal is in some degree of discomfort or because the owners are not sure what is wrong with their pet. They are there because the owner perceives it is an emergency. It is our job to identify the problem, insure that it is not life threatening, and to calm the owner's fears.

"Really?" I want to say to people when they show up in the middle of the night and pay an exorbitant ER exam fee just for me to treat a small wound that they probably would have slapped a Band-Aid on if it was on their own body. I have to admit though, that injuries can sometimes look worse than they actually are. On one of my shifts, a dog arrived who had once been a fuzzy white dog. But now the dog was a fuzzy red dog. From head to toe the dog was stained red in color. He was joyously panting and victoriously bouncing around the room. Despite his startling appearance of having been massacred, he was obviously not in any distress.

"What happened?" I asked a little worried myself by his dramatic fur color change.

"He was in a fight with a beaver," the owner told me.

Ah, the old 'Bit By Beaver' syndrome. Now there's something we don't see very often on ER. This must have been a very fierce beaver with which the dog had decided to tussle. Under sedation, I proceeded to clip around the blood-covered dog's wounds. When shaved down, the total damage amounted to a large number of superficial scratches and shallow tooth scrapes all over his body. An impressive sight to see, but once cleaned up not a very impressive medical problem at all.

On a different evening that summer, another animal attack victim showed up at my hospital. This time it was a cat named Percy. Percy was a relaxed, somewhat indignant looking, flat-faced Persian who had small punctures all over his nose and ears.

"What happened to Percy?" I assumed the owner would answer, "a cat fight," which is the most common cause of feline wounds.

"He was attacked by our hamster," Percy's owner told me.

Now I myself have experienced the wrath of a pissed off hamster so I knew not to negate the potential fierceness of these creatures. Adorable on first appearance, fuzzy sweet-faced hamsters can be quite quick and purposeful with their teeth when given a reason. The cat in front of me apparently had not made any attempt to defend himself when the hamster attacked. In front of me sat a born rodent killer who had just been severely humiliated by a tiny rodent. We clipped the fur around his face leaving his neck fur intact. When we were done, Percy looked like a sickly vulture. This did nothing to restore Percy's dignity.

"Don't worry Percy," I whispered to him as he left, "your secret is safe with us. We'll just tell everyone it was a large raccoon that beat you up, and that you fought valiantly."

The never-ending assortment of animals or objects with which pets tussle never ceases to amaze me. One evening Janet, our local dog officer, walked in the door carrying a cocktail table which normally resides in a family room. *There is nothing I can do to help that thing*, I thought to myself, *it is already dead*. On second glance, I realized that firmly attached to the table, and also in the hands of the officer, was a ten pound dog. Somehow the dog had managed to jam its leg into one of the small bends in the table's flouncy wrought iron legs. His leg was now so swollen that nobody could extract him. Any attempts to free his leg would result in the dog screaming in ear-piercing shrieks. Even with sedation, the table still wasn't budging without risk of breaking the dog's tiny leg. In desperation we called the local fire department who was nice enough to come by and cut the iron-legged table off. The little dog left walking with a limp but he seemed happy to be free of his unwanted date – the family cocktail table.

Other entanglement cases occur more naturally. Occasionally a puzzled owner will show up with what we call a "kitten ball." This occurs when a pregnant cat has snuck off and given birth in some hidden corner of their property. Six or seven kittens are born in rapid succession with their umbilical cords still attached to the placenta. As the kittens crawl all over each other they entangle each other up in the cords. From a far distance, this tangle of kittens gives the impression of a writhing round mass of undulating fur. One kitten's nose is tightly pinned to the next kittens belly, this kitten is tied in a folded over position, and the next kitten's front foot is stuffed into the next kitten's mouth. They are weaved into a tightly knit ball and are vocalizing but are unable to move. The only way to rectify the situation is to patiently clip each cord as close to the umbilicus as possible in an attempt to free up its associated kitten. It is harder than you would expect, as it would be easy to inadvertently remove a tiny foot or toe. There are usually casualties from a kitten ball. If a cord has wrapped itself around a kitten's leg, then the limb may be strangulated. If the blood supply has been compromised for a long enough time, the limb will eventually fall off leaving the kitten without an arm or a leg. Felines are a tenacious species and most of the kittens, even those lacking a limb, usually go on to thrive.

We see a wide variety of animals on our emergency shifts. We don't have the luxury of consulting with a zoo veterinarian when the owners show up late on a Saturday evening. I've treated snakes, bearded dragons, hedge hogs, sugar gliders, hawks, deer, goats, pigs, and companion birds. But one day something new arrived on my emergency shift. A wallaroo baby named Pugsley. A wallaroo is a creature which is half-way in size between a wallaby and a kangaroo. They grow to about fifty pounds. This wallaroo was brought in because he had a stress attack after being relocated to his new pen. Apparently stress is a common cause of illness in marsupials. This little guy's overwhelming unhappiness with his new surroundings caused him to faint and lose oxygen to his brain. He woke up with stroke-like symptoms and was blind.

Now I do not know the first thing about wallaroos, other than they look cute in photos of the Australian outback. I did not have a clue as to how to treat Pugsley for his panic attack and couldn't think of a single medication or certified wallaroo psychologist who could help him. Luckily, veterinary resources are now available via the internet and these offered me some basic medical advice. I feel dearly for my predecessors who, before the advent of the internet, were forced to treat unusual medical problems or exotic pets by gut instinct alone. Pugsley's owner ran a petting zoo and was quite knowledgeable about the medical diseases of wallaroos. He gave me a few important tips and then left Pugsley with us overnight so that he could get human interaction and affection throughout the night. I was worried that a hospital environment would create even more stress for Pugsley but the owner, who had to leave out of town that night, felt that Pugsley was so people-bound that this was the best means of keeping him calm.

He dropped Pugsley off in a handmade cotton pouch which the wallaroo literally hung around in. We hung the pouch from one of our IV stands where Pugsley contentedly swung while passively chewing on his hay. Pugsley seemed to be coping well with his recent blindness. No one had to twist our arms to give this Roo some extra loving. We took turns holding him throughout the night. What a lucky person I am. Who else, short of people living in the outback or zoo keepers, gets to play with an orphaned kangaroo baby all night? The answer is we do, we do...the members of an emergency veterinary team.

The rewards of my job also come through the interactions that I witness between my clients. One memorable evening, a young man rushed into our hospital carrying a limp, wet body covered in black and white fur. The sopping wet creature was barely identifiable as a cat. The man was ashen-faced and frightened.

"I let my dog out to go to the bathroom before bed and suddenly he lunged at something in the darkness. The next thing I knew he was attacking this cat who was trying to scramble under the car."

He passed the soggy body over to me and I could see that the cat was breathing but very shallowly. The man couldn't have been more than twenty-five, was well-muscled, and tattooed down both arms. He knew that by most city laws all dogs should be confined. He also knew that since he owned a pitbull, a breed with a public image of ferociousness, authorities can be particularly harsh. Their reputation is so fierce that insurance companies in some states will not provide home insurance to people if they own this breed. I would argue that this image is somewhat unfair but that's a whole different story.

We treated the kitty for shock and pain. The young man had already indicated that he was willing to pay for the medical care of the cat, but for a few reasons I was skeptical that this would actually happen. First, traumas such as this are often quite extensive. It can take several hours and sometimes days to realize the full extent of the damage. Extensive surgeries may be needed to repair the damage as we become aware of it. The good Samaritan who brings in an attacked animal usually has the best of intentions but is somewhat naïve about the degree of damage or how rapidly the bill is going to rise. These traumas can easily end up costing into the thousands and, even with the best medical care, a fair number of attack victims will not survive the days ahead.

Second, this was a young kid. I doubt he had $100 saved in the bank, never mind enough to finance a major medical trauma. Third, he didn't own the cat and he didn't have a lot of emotional attachment to it. These situations often end with an angry confrontation between the owner of the injured pet and the owner of the animal that attacked it.

This lucky cat had a collar on with identification. Most end up as an unknown body in our freezer. I called the number and a worried voice came over the other end.

"Oh thank God you've found Mr. Bo Jingles," she said. She went on to tell me that he's purely an indoor cat and he snuck out the front door a day ago. They had been looking for him ever since.

"We were frightened for him. He has never been out and it's rainy and cold. Do everything you can for him. We'll be right down." I reflected on how amazing it was that an indoor cat had a collar with tags on it. This must be a very loved cat indeed.

The owner came down with four children in tow…one baby in a stroller, two toddlers and a young boy of about eight. They were all in their pajamas. *Great,* I thought to myself, prejudging the situation once again, *a single mom with four kids. She's not going to have the ability to fund this either. This is going to get ugly quickly.* Despite the obvious cause of this cat's injuries, if the dog owner could not come up with the cash to pay the bill, then the cat owner was ultimately the one responsible for payment that night. And when push comes to shove, it is difficult to get law officials to enforce payment.

The woman and the young tattooed man faced each other for the first time. He had the guilty look of someone who has done something wrong. She looked pissed off and upset. I went into the back to tend to Bo Jingles. I didn't want to be around for the upcoming encounter between them. Luckily it was late and there were no other clients in the front room to witness the melee.

I returned thirty minutes later. I tentatively peeked into the lobby to see if there had been any bloodshed. To my surprise the children were curled up napping. The woman and the young man were calmly sipping coffee and amicably sharing pet stories. I gave them an update on Bo Jingles, who seemed to be slowly coming around. His temperature was warming, his back wasn't broken, his diaphragm wasn't ruptured, his bladder was intact, he was not bleeding internally. He had minor lung contusions and at this point, none of his wounds seemed overly extensive. He was quite lucky really, one of the few to have survived an attack by a dog and not have major injuries. If he continued to do well, the bill would probably be a few hundred, but not a few thousand. A look of relief passed over both of their faces. Hers because she believed her cat would live, and his because his bank account wouldn't be depleted and he wasn't going to end up in a court of law.

They walked up to the front desk continuing their chat. Then they each pulled out a credit card and split the estimated bill. I couldn't believe it. They were going to share the bill and they both could afford it. None of this was normal at an ER hospital. She was going to pay her half because she accepted her part of the responsibility in this, which was letting her indoor, declawed cat escape outside. He was going to pay his half because he accepted his responsibility in this encounter, which is that his dog was off of the leash. The owners actually seemed to be bonding. Go figure, friendship instead of anger, acceptance of responsibility instead of blame, neighborliness instead of antagonism. What a concept, if only others in the world could witness this olive branch being passed between them. For sure, my faith in the goodness of people was refreshed that night.

CHAPTER 15

A VOLATILE BUSINESS

It is 3:00 in the morning and my two technicians, Shelly and Bree, are straddling a 180 pound Great Dane that is lying on the floor as they change his bandages. The dog is large enough that one person can easily straddle him from the back end and the other one at his front end, with plenty of room in between. As I walk around the dog, all I can see are two human butts sticking up in the air. Both ladies' scrub pants have dropped around their hips and one butt reveals a red thong climbing up her well exposed butt crack and the other has lace pink panties visible in almost their entirety. Scrub pants, as comfortable as they are, are not utilitarian outfits. With their flimsy string waist cord, they are definitely not properly constructed for bending over. Something that most veterinary technicians spend a large amount of time doing.

Not being able to restrain myself, I crack out loud, "Is this a strip club or a veterinary hospital?"

I am half joking and half serious, as there did seem to be a large number of butt cracks and underwear visible amongst the younger generation of technicians. It is more than I could remember seeing in my early years of practice and doesn't paint a very professional appearance when clients come through the hospital. It was happening so frequently lately that the hospital manager had felt the need to send out a carefully worded e-mail asking employees to be "careful with exposure of their undergarments." I knew that my male colleagues would never have the nerve to say anything to the ladies. At least I hope they wouldn't.

They both giggle coquettishly. "It can be anything you want it to be," they reply.

They follow this comment by simultaneously lifting their bottoms and waving their bottoms in the air to demonstrate their adept strip-dancing capabilities. Anything goes when it is 3:00 in the morning and everyone is punch silly. I know equally as well that they would never have the nerve to dance like that in front of my male associates. At least I hope these technicians wouldn't.

"It wouldn't be so bad if there wasn't a butt crack facing me in whatever direction I walk," I lightly reprimand them again, but I walk away with a grin on my face.

This is a tough job, they deserve some fun. The back doorbell rings. As the ladies are inconveniently straddling a giant dog while dual pole dancing, they ask me to answer it.

"It's probably Helen stuck outside with an uncooperative dog."

The rear door to the hospital is a solid metal one which leads out to a poorly lit parking lot in the back. Our hospital is stationed in one of the seediest districts in town. Veterinary hospitals are high risk businesses for armed robbery or other felonies as they contain a large supply of controlled drugs, a stash of cash and, usually, a large assortment of young and pretty women. Since there has never been a problem at this hospital, our wariness has tended to fade with time.

I open the heavy door to find a large man, wearing a hooded sweatshirt, at arm's length in front of me. It's raining lightly and his hood is pulled up over his head. The unexpected sight of him, instead of Helen, at the door takes me off guard. My immediate reflex is to scream, and scream I do, as loudly as I can and directly into his face. My reaction must be as unexpected to him as his presence at the door is to me. The man retorts by screaming equally as loud and as long, jumping back and dropping the paperwork that he is carrying in his hands. Not to be outdone, I scream again. We both stop in dead silence, face to face with each other's frightened expressions, and start laughing uncontrollably. In the background I can see my technician running for a phone.

"Why you do that? Why you do that?" the man repeats over and over again holding his hand over his heart which, I assume, is his attempt to stop its rapid beating. He is foreign and his English is stilted. His hand is on the doorway blocking me from closing the door.

"You scared the hell out of me, that's why. Why are you here at my back door at 3 am?" I retort.

I am wary and realize how vulnerable I am, standing in the door with him just a few inches from me. It wouldn't take much for him to push past me and he would be in the back hallway. If he was truly here for criminal reasons and had a gun in his pocket, what difference would it make if we had our hands on the telephone? His eyes keep glancing back to the technicians and the phone that they are holding in his full view.

"I need to make delivery. It open here. Where this address?"

He points to a work order for a delivery of a supply of doors to a warehouse a few doors down. It still doesn't explain why he is here in the wee hours of the morning. Over his shoulder I can see a large truck in our parking lot and I note that his paperwork truly does have a delivery address for the building down the road. At least his story fits. I point him in the right direction and shut the door as fast as I can. My heart is beating loudly with fright at the recognition of how bad this situation could have been.

I relay the story to my manager the next day.

"What a creep," she replies, "who comes to the back door of a business at 3 am?"

Well, in this case a lost foreign delivery man who doesn't have enough social skills to realize that entering a back door in the dark of night is not an appropriate choice. But it could have been any sicko or violent perpetrator for whom I had inadvertently opened the door. We discuss safety issues that should be instituted including a peephole in the door, panic buttons, video surveillance, and alerting the police that this is a high-risk business for armed robbery or other felonies. The hospital had already improved the lighting outside and instituted a policy that at night all employees should walk outside with a buddy and with a mobile panic button. We also discussed organizing a training session on what to do in the event of an emergency.

Janet further points out that this is a volatile business and the nature of our business means that there will be very irate clients. She cautioned that "we can only do so much to protect people here. That is why you and the staff have to by hyperaware and take protective steps yourselves. I had a crazy on the phone last week who was angry about the care his pet received. His threats were so violent that I had to have our lawyer write him a letter preventing him from calling any more. People become very emotional about their animals, particularly if the outcome isn't how they wished. Who's to stop some guy from walking in here with a machine gun and just start shooting? We can't wear protective vests all day long."

Some days protective vests seem like a good idea. One busy Sunday we were working diligently to see the mass of incoming patients. Around 2:00 in the afternoon, a technician brought a young female pug, who was in dystocia, into the back treatment area. Dystocia is the medical term we use for the inability of an animal to naturally pass their offspring. This frightened young dog had a puppy tightly lodged in her vulva with its body halfway out. The puppy's tail and hind legs were hanging out behind her like some aberrant appendage. The puppy's legs would move when I touched them so I knew it was still alive. I glanced out to the exam room area and I could see that every room was filled with clients who had probably already waited an hour or more.

This truly was an emergency. If I did not stop and help the pup then it may die and if left long enough, the mother's uterus might tear and she may die as well. Besides sincerely wanting to help the dog and the puppy, there were legal implications to not helping her right away. Breeders are notorious for filing lawsuits against veterinarians especially if they think the veterinarian did not deliver the puppies in a timely enough fashion. I know several veterinarians who have been sued over cesarean sections or their pregnancy management that had resulted in the deaths of valuable pups. At $800 to $1400 a pup, it was no small change and many back-yard breeders breed for one reason only, money.

While the technicians went up front to talk to the owner and have him fill out the requisite paperwork, I started to work on getting the stuck pup out. I couldn't stand to see the mother dog in that much distress, and I couldn't watch the wriggling hind end of the pup any longer. If the amniotic sac surrounding the puppy's face had already ruptured, then every minute counted. I was conscious that this would delay me seeing the rooms for probably thirty minutes, which would make for a whole bunch of cranky owners waiting in a tiny square room, oblivious to what was happening in the back of the hospital.

To my surprise, the pup came out with moderate ease. A little lubrication, hand holds in the right place, coordinated gentle pulls, and I was able to ease the pup out into the world alive. I cleared the pup's mouth of secretions, dried it off, warmed it up, and stimulated it to breathe. The mother dog looked relieved and was struggling to get out of the hands of the technician in order to lick her newborn. In the midst of caring for the first pup, contractions began again and a second puppy started to emerge. I waited around, concerned that this one too might get stuck, but within a matter of a few minutes, the second pup made it out with little assistance needed on my part. *This owner is going to be thrilled,* I thought. We successfully extracted the two healthy pups without a dangerous anesthetic to the mom and pups, or a costly cesarean section. I tallied up the bill which came to a mere $129, which included the exam and a birthing assist. I was trying to hurry, as my front room technician, Willie, kept popping back to remind me about the impatient clients in the rooms.

I sent Willie up front to touch base with the owner. In the meantime, I went into the room where clients had been waiting the longest. After finishing with them, the receptionist informed me that the owner of the pug was refusing to pay his bill. I went up to the reception area to see what the issue was.

The owner was a tall, thin, sour-faced man, wearing a plaid shirt and jeans.

"I'm not paying that," the man spit out in an angry, curt fashion.

"Why not?" I asked, perplexed.

"I never signed anything saying that I would pay that," he said. He had me there. I had delivered the stuck puppy before he had officially signed the incoming papers.

"But what did you bring your dog in for?" I asked puzzled. "She had a puppy hanging out of her bottom."

"I wanted to speak to you first. I am not paying that. Give me my dog!" His tone and mannerisms were becoming louder and more agitated.

This was ridiculous. It was true that I hadn't spoken to him on presentation, but he walked into an ER hospital with a distressed dog and a stuck puppy, and handed it off to a technician for us to care for. What was he expecting us to do? Vaccinate her and hand her back? I was suspecting that this guy was just trying to get out of paying his bill. I ushered him into the pharmacy area to get him out of sight and sound of the reception area clients.

"Listen," I started again speaking softly and trying to calm him down and reason with him. I figured I could talk to him, educate him, explain what we had done and explain why the costs had been incurred. Few people are that unreasonable.

There was no rationalizing with this man.

"Just give my dog and my puppies," he said. "I never gave you permission to do anything to my dog."

It was as if he knew the legalities of treating pets, as if he had done something like this before. He started to push past me through the swinging doors into the prep room which was clearly marked, *Employees Only*. Legally, we didn't have the right to hold his dog but he certainly wasn't going to just stroll into the back of our hospital and grab his dog. People just don't do that. He would need to sign a financial agreement for the services we had rendered.

I positioned myself in front of the swinging door as a visual deterrent and in a last attempt to try and reason with him. That didn't stop him. The man pushed past me and, in the process, I was forced into the adjacent wall. That was more than my technician, Willlie, could bear. Willie was a round butterball of a man, but he prided himself on once having been a security guard. Despite his round appearance, he was a powerful guy. He also had a strong sense of chivalry and didn't like seeing his female doctor pushed into a wall. Willie jumped in front of the man and they were quickly immersed in shoving each other back and forth and exchanging loud words like two high school football players in the locker room. I knew that Willie's response was a bit overboard for the situation, but I couldn't do anything to stop him. Teresa, a young, pretty ER doctor, tried to jump in the middle of them, assuming that they wouldn't hit her.

"Whoa boys, whoa," she said putting her hands up in front of them.

But it was fruitless. The situation was escalating and the two men were now exchanging blows. The noise was loud enough to attract the attention of the clients in the two exam rooms adjacent to the hallway. One client from each of the rooms emerged and jumped into the progressing melee. I was horrified that clients were now involved in this situation. They pinned the angry owner to one wall, while Teresa held Willie against the other wall.

I ran into the back and grabbed his dog and her two puppies and brought them back to the pharmacy area where the angry crowd was gathered.

"Here. Here is your dog. Just leave the premises," I told him shoving the dog and the pups into his hands. Nothing was worth this. I wanted this crazy man out so I could attend to my other clients at the hospital. I didn't want a scene like this on my ER shift over something so stupid. It's disturbing to other clients and bad for business.

The clients let go of the man, who took his dog and the puppies from me and stormed out of the building. In the background, I noticed a frightened technician speaking on the phone giving out his description to the police. We all calmed ourselves and fixed our disheveled clothing. I walked into the room of one of the clients who had helped to break up the tussle to thank him and apologize for the disturbance. He was a long-haired, hippie-looking dude.

"I heard the whole thing," he said. "What was he expecting you to do when he walked in with his dog trying to give birth? What an idiot," he stated over and over again, "what an idiot."

He was expressing the exact sentiments that I, in an attempt to remain professional, had been reluctant to say out loud. I tried to focus my attention on his dog that he had brought in for lameness. I talked with him throughout the examination, all the while trying to pretend that this was just a regular day at a veterinary ER hospital. The rooms were now filled with pissed-off clients who had been waiting for over an hour.

"I thought you must have gone off on lunch break," was the first thing the frustrated owner in the next room said to me.

"I am sorry for the delay. Poor Fluffy, having to sit here all this time with a broken nail," I replied with my most believable and sympathetic smile.

I continued on, thoroughly examining Fluffy's toenail and giving it the medical attention that she expected. I continued chatting amicably to her. I tried as best I could to soothe her anger and to smooth out the situation so that she would only remember her visit to our hospital as a pleasurable one.

CHAPTER 16

CANDY AND CONDOMS

"A transfer is coming over from Dr. Snell," said the intern who was working when I arrived for my evening shift. "It's a Gummy Bear toxicity."

I glanced at her to see if she was kidding. There is no such thing as a Gummy Bear toxicity, or a cinnamon lip toxicity, or a candy corn toxicity for that matter.

"She's kidding," I told the intern.

Knowing Dr. Snell, she was just toying with our intern. Dr. Snell was a quick witted Easterner with a wry sense of humor. She probably meant that the dog had eaten some candies and now was vomiting or had bad diarrhea, which is the most common sequelae to eating inappropriate things. To be sure that I wasn't missing something in my education, I went to the computer to search the literature. I typed the words, **Gummy Bear toxicity,** into the on-line veterinary resource site. To my surprise, several references appeared on the screen.

"The high corn syrup acts to create an osmotic diarrhea. High sodium levels may result and can lead to seizures, coma or death," read the veterinary abstract.

Go figure, death by Gummy Bears. In layman's terms, the article states that if ingested in high enough quantities, the thick nature of corn syrup may cause excessive water to leave your cells. This results in a high level of salt in your bloodstream. This excessively high salt level can have serious or potentially fatal consequences.

Griffin, an elderly Jack Russell Terrier, arrived at our hospital transferred from Dr. Snell's office. Griffin didn't look good when he arrived. He was lying on the table, groaning in discomfort. His belly was swollen and he would moan when you touched him. I knew that I could help him with his belly ache symptoms, but if he suddenly developed high sodium levels he would have big problems that are much more difficult to treat. I was curious as to what had inspired a fifteen-year-old, half senile dog to eat a pound of Gummy Bears.

"Has he ever eaten unusual things before?" I asked the owner.

"No," she replied through tears, "he actually broke into the cabinet this morning to get at the bag."

A dog after my own heart, I thought. Gummy bears are a staple in our household. I usually have a large bag of them in the cupboard. I like to eat them with breakfast, after lunch, and sometimes for dinner, and then after dinner too. *Gummy bears make everything better,* is one of my favorite lines and my excuse to reach for them when the day is getting bad. My boyfriend would jokingly ask me to please do him the favor of letting him know if my urine ever turned multicolored so that he could get me to the doctor for an early intervention. Well here it was in flesh and blood, in my own hospital, my first patient with a case of Gummy Bearitis.

Over the course of the next hour, Griffin started to look worse. He became progressively more unresponsive and a rapid twitch started to develop in his hind legs. I rechecked his blood work and his sodium had climbed quite a few points in the last few hours. It is the rapid changes in sodium levels in your bloodstream that will create the most serious problem. Salt toxicity as it is more commonly known in layman's terms may start as twitching, progress to diffuse tremors or full blown seizures and in worst case scenarios can lead to coma or death. I switched the type of fluid that Griffin was receiving in an attempt to drop his sodium levels at a slow rate. Luckily for Griffin the fluid therapy worked and over the course of the evening his mentation improved and he began to sit up and look like a healthy dog again. Panting and smug, his appearance gave the impression of *don't you dare reprimand me. I'm a senior citizen and if I want to eat Gummy Bears, then I damn well will.* Belly ache or not, it seemed to have been worth it for him. I completely understood.

That morning in rounds I transferred Griffin over to the team of veterinary specialists who would be taking over his care.

"Griffin is a fifteen-year-old, male, neutered Jack Russell being treated for Gummy Bear toxicity," I confidently told them. The smiles and giggles that erupted amongst them reaffirmed that they, too, had never heard of this disease. I could tell that they were doubting my diagnosis.

"Go look it up," I told them.

I was feeling gleeful that I had finally stumped this bright group of doctors with a medical condition that they were not aware of.

Candy ingestion is not an uncommon scenario in the veterinary world. In the emergency room we see a lot of chocolate-eating dogs. Christmas, Halloween, and Valentine's Day are all bad holidays for chocolate-loving dogs of the world. In mild cases it will cause gastrointestinal signs like vomiting or diarrhea, but sometimes it will cause more serious problems such as excessively high heart rates, hyperactivity or seizures. Although severe side effects are rare, it is the one potential toxin that owners seem to be hyper-vigilant about. Owners will rush their dog down to our ER hospital even if their pet has only licked a chocolate-flavored food item. I have spent a countless number of hours trying to calm panicked owners of chocolate-eating dogs by assuring them that the likelihood their dog will live is really quite high.

One nauseous-looking chocolate-eater vomited three pounds of wrapped Halloween candy in my office. We verified this by reweighing him after he had finished vomiting. Wave after wave of vomit-covered Hersheys, followed by vomit-covered Milky Ways, vomit-covered Reeses and then a wave of gooey foil-covered marshmallow ghosts came out of the mouth of this now somewhat regretful looking Labrador Retriever. I was trying hard not to vomit up my own lunch after visualizing this large and colorful pile of brown goo.

Typically, if an animal has eaten something inappropriate, we will give it an injection which forces it to vomit. The vomiting that is induced is fairly violent and causes repeated waves of heaving. After it has emptied its stomach, we wrap the dog in a towel and then we administer a large volume of charcoal into its mouth. This thick, black, liquid charcoal is intended to prevent further absorption of whatever it has eaten. It is an unpleasant and messy experience for everyone involved. By the end of the charcoal procedure the technician, the dog, and the hospital all look as if they've been finger painted with the black substance. And the dog looks as if all it wants to do is get as far away as possible from this crazy group of people.

Candy isn't the only inappropriate substance animals will try to eat. I was typing records one Saturday afternoon when my triage technician announced that there was a couple up front whose cat had eaten their condom. *Yuck,* I thought, imagining having to clean that up after we forced the cat to vomit.

"I recognize the guy, he's the running back for the local college football team," my sports-loving technician, Sean, told me.

The local college team was on a winning streak and highly ranked in the country that year. It had set the city and the state on fire. Personally I'm not a football fan, but it was fun to work with a local celebrity, even if it had to do with his used condoms.

"He's with his girlfriend," Sean said, "and she looks like a people person to me." He made the motion of quotation marks with his fingers as he used the term 'people person'. He was referencing the fact that he felt the girl was overly friendly with the boys.

"Wait a minute there, he must be a 'people person' too for them to both be here in this predicament," I retorted refusing to allow the female half to be placed as the only promiscuous one in this scenario.

"It's gonna be an extra-large condom too," Sean blurted out with yet another inappropriate and stereotypical comment about football players.

I went up front to explain to the amorous couple what I needed to do for their kitten. These were always awkward conversations, as I found talking about condoms and indirectly about their sex life uncomfortable.

I figured I should just get it out up front. "So I understand your kitten ate your condom?"

I was waiting for a smile or a giggle or something to lighten the moment but it didn't come. They both just sat there looking sheepish and then nodded their heads silently.

Looking at the couple I had to admit that maybe Sean was right on this one. She did kind of look like a 'people person', bleached hair, tight clothing, big booty, excessive makeup, and a plastered-on smile adorned with hot pink lipstick. I'm all for women experiencing life, but this lady had the appearance that all she cared about was the prestige of being associated with a quasi-famous college football player.

"I need to try to get your kitten to vomit and if we can't do that, then we may need to pass an endoscope into his stomach and try to retrieve it so it doesn't get stuck in his intestines." They both nodded their heads again – apparently these two could screw, but were unable to speak.

We brought the kitten to the back and gave it a drug to induce vomiting. We all watched in sick fascination as a bright-blue-colored condom erupted from its mouth in what seemed like slow motion.

"Gross," we muttered in unison. Figures…team colors too.

"Don't throw that away. I'll go check to see if they want that back," I winked to my technicians as I ran up front to let the couple know that we had successfully retrieved their love object.

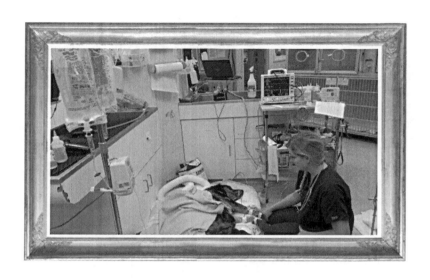

CHAPTER 17

GAMBLING

It is 3:00 in the morning. A phone call comes in to our hospital from one of our well-loved ER technicians named Andrea.

"It's Autumn. She's in a lot of pain. I think she's bloating." Muffled sobs follow her words.

"I'm coming down. We'll be there in twenty minutes." A click and a dial tone follow.

Autumn is a vibrant and bouncy three-year-old Boxer. She is Andrea's constant companion. From Andrea's tearful phone-call, I suspect that Autumn will not be bouncing when she arrives through our doors. This time Autumn will arrive with her belly so swollen and so tautly distended from her condition, that she will be pacing and loudly retching in a feeble attempt to relieve the unbearable tension from air which is rapidly growing within her abdomen.

In the veterinary profession, bloat is the slang word for when a dog's stomach physically twists one hundred and eighty degrees within the abdominal cavity. The effect of this twisting action is that air and fluid buildup within the walls of the stomach until it distends to its rupturing point. The poor dog who is affected by this condition is experiencing an unbearable amount of pain.

It will arrive at our hospital trying to cope with the worst case of gas colic that one can imagine. The owners also arrive frantic with worry after having being woken up in the early hours of the morning by their distraught pet begging them for help.

Bloat is one of those medical words that sends my veterinary staff into immediate action in preparation for the animal's arrival. Upon the dog's arrival at our hospital, our first concern is to alleviate its pain and when that is accomplished, we place an IV line in an effort to stabilize his soon-to-be-crashing blood pressure. Once these stabilizing methods are in place, I proceed with one of the more dramatic therapies that we have in veterinary medicine. Using a long wide bore needle, I place its point at the dog's side and forcefully pop it into the animal's taut stomach wall. The reward comes when we hear a hiss of air rushing out through the needle. This sound is the confirmation that I have placed my needle correctly into the gas-distended lumen of his stomach. In an almost equally dramatic response, the dog's swollen belly deflates in front of us. I have accomplished my immediate goal, which is to relieve this animal's pain and to relieve the unrelenting pressure building up within his belly. But I know that this relief will only be short-lived if we do not get him to surgery immediately to untwist his torqued stomach which is rapidly distending with air as we wait. Nothing but surgery will help this pup.

After I have stabilized my patient, my next most pressing job is to stabilize the frightened owners. First, I explain what is happening to their pet, whose body is eerily metamorphosing in front of them, and then I attempt to calm them. I need for them to be coherent so they will understand my next words fully. I need for them to be able to make rational decisions because what I have to say next will shatter this family's happy existence.

In a calm and succinct manner I explain to them that their dog's stomach has flipped into the wrong anatomic location. A Gastric Dilatation Volvulus is the official medical term for what the layman calls a bloat. I explain that in order to save their pet's life it will need to be brought immediately to surgery. I explain that this decision needs to be made rapidly in the next quarter of an hour because even as we speak the sequence of events that brought them here tonight is repeating itself. If their reasoning paths are heading away from the path of surgery, then I must start the next phase of this dance and begin preparing them for the decisions they will have to make to euthanize their pet who was healthy three hours ago.

The only good news in this situations is the statistics involved with performing this surgery. If done with the proper surgical know-how, and with the proper post-operative care, eighty-five percent of these dogs will survive a stomach volvulus and live a normal life thereafter. By a gambler's way of thinking, those odds are in their favor.

Andrea arrives with Autumn. Autumn was named for the season that that she was adopted in. It is obvious that Autumn is not doing well. Her gums are pale, she is profoundly weak, and her belly is swollen and firm. Her temperature is four degrees below normal and her blood pressure is too low to register. She lies on the examination table writhing in pain. I give her pain medications and bolus her fluids in an attempt to improve her frighteningly low blood pressure. Her blood pressure climbs but it is a short-lived victory as it rapidly bottoms back out to its starting point.

Watching your dog decompensate and in an escalating level of pain is scary. It is particularly frightening when you are a member of the profession and are aware of everything that can go wrong. The technicians we have at our veterinary hospital are highly knowledgeable and technically skilled. They remain in a difficult and physically demanding job because they care. Yet despite all of the skills and hard work of a veterinary technician, the profession remains poorly paid. Few technicians are financially prepared to pay for such a surgery. Yet the reason they chose this line of work in the first place is because they are willing to go to the end of the earth and to the bottom of their bank account in order to help their pet if the need arises.

I ask for x-rays to be taken of Autumn. The results are not what we expected. This is not a stomach volvulus. In this case, Autumn's belly is distended for a more ominous reason. There is fluid leaking from her intestines, causing her abdomen to look swollen. When the intestines leak, all of the bacteria that is normally contained within them will float free in the belly, creating a horrifically painful infection called a peritonitis. Even with the most aggressive medical and surgical intervention, peritonitis is a very difficult disease to survive.

I phone the surgeon on call to come down immediately. The hospital where I work is called a referral hospital, which means that it is staffed with veterinarians who have completed a residency in a specific field of veterinary medicine. In this case I call in a veterinarian who had completed an additional four-year residency in the practice of surgery. Over the phone I relay Autumn's symptoms to him. I try to speak distinctly and with emphasis as I know he was fast asleep when he answered my call. I need him to comprehend my words so that he can react quickly. I need for him to hear the urgency in my voice so I can motivate him to get down here as quickly as possible.

The room is silent as we work on Autumn. Everyone, including Andrea, is aware that this is not going in the direction we want. The ring of the doorbell alerts us to another client arriving. It is a woman and her young daughter carrying a Golden Retriever puppy. They have been awakened by the whimpers of their puppy who was sadly holding up his front leg at their home. I reluctantly leave Autumn to see them. I am hoping that this will be brief. Right now Autumn needs my full attention. In the exam room the puppy is bounding around without a perceivable limp. At first glance I intuitively know that this puppy is just fine. Puppies tend to be quite dramatic in their responses to pain. Mild injuries will result in major reactions. I examine the puppy trying not to give the impression of being rushed. The woman winces and cries out herself when I start to feel her puppy's leg. An overly concerned expression arises on her face. I explain to the woman that her puppy's responses may be a bit overdone for the extent of the injury that it has.

The woman glances lovingly at her young daughter and tells me, "My eight year old daughter has that same problem."

After observing the mothers responses to my exam, and factor in her need to pay an emergency fee at 4:00 in the morning for a minor lameness, I know exactly why her daughter has a tendency to over dramatize things. Just like pets, children will mimic the reactions and emotions of the parental figures in their lives. I offer the woman the option of having x-rays taken of her puppy's leg. I silently pray that she will defer this test. Right now I need my technicians to help with Autumn who is in a critical state. No such luck. The woman is insistent on having the x-rays taken. She has just arrived in the wee hours of the morning and her puppy's lameness is an emergency to her. The old adage that an emergency is in the eyes of the owner holds true. I unwrap the nervous puppy from her arms. She is clinging to him like he is a fragile doll. I am willing to bet my week's salary that the x-rays are going to be normal.

Autumn's heart rate is now over 170. Two strong doses of morphine have not abated her pain. She is now so weak she can no longer lift her head. The proteins in her blood are being lost so rapidly that I need to transfuse her with plasma to improve her blood pressure and enhance her ability to clot. Her temperature continues to decline. Despite all of our therapies, Autumn is getting worse, not better. Autumn is trying to die. Andrea is silent and willfully refusing to accept what is obvious to the rest of us. We move Autumn into the operating room and scrub her in preparation for the surgeon's arrival.

The puppy's x-rays do not show any orthopedic problems. His lameness may be from a bruise or a muscle strain. I make up pain medications for the woman to take home. When I return to the room, the woman again tries to convince me of the severity of his problem. She repeats his symptoms telling me that he never does these things. I wonder about her use of the word 'never', as she has only owned him three weeks. I patiently re-explain how puppies often have dramatic responses to pain and reassure her that he is practically normal now. While I am speaking, the puppy rummages through our garbage can...a telltale sign that his leg can't be hurting him too badly.

I try to extract myself by explaining that I have a critical patient in the back that needs my attention. This doesn't deter her at all. Could I examine his neck where he has an area of hair loss? She is certain the hair loss is being caused by fleas. And if he does have fleas, what can she do about it? This is her emergency, and she is paying an emergency fee so that I will give her puppy my full and undivided attention. It is her way of proving how much she loves her puppy. It doesn't matter to her that these are not problems that need to be addressed at an emergency hospital at 4:00 in the morning, and that I have a dying patient in the back.

I get away, feeling frustrated and angry. I remind myself that critical emergency or not, this is part of my job and my job involves reassuring people that their mildly ill or mildly hurt pet will be okay. Yet it is difficult to empathize with this type of energy-sucking client. I would like to see how this dramatic woman behaves when her pet has a true emergency which requires my undivided attention. Most likely she will not be very tolerant of me spending time in the next room with an owner discussing their dog's flea problem.

The surgeon arrives as quickly as he can but in what seems like an interminable amount of time to those of us waiting. I repeat to him what is going on with Autumn and what we have done to stabilize her, as I am not sure how much he comprehended in his half-conscious state on the phone.

"Her pain is unmanageable, her temperature has dropped to ninety-one, and her blood pressure continues to plummet despite aggressive therapeutics."

We exchange a look that shares our innermost thoughts. This is going to be something bad. I scrub in behind him because I know he's going to need a second hand.

On the initial incision into the abdomen we both immediately know that Autumn will probably not survive. It is what veterinarians call a 'peek and shriek' moment. You look into the surgical area and things appear so ugly that you want to close up and go back to bed and pretend it didn't happen. Her intestines are ominously black from one end to the other. Hemorrhagic fluid wells up from her belly.

We exteriorize her intestines and find that, as a whole group, they have twisted themselves into a knot. We didn't expect this. This is a different kind of torsion…a much, much worse one. This is called a mesenteric torsion. This poorly understood spontaneous hundred and eighty degree twisting of the entire length of the bowels results in a loss of blood flow to the entire intestinal tract. Without blood, the intestinal loops will quickly die. It is a rare condition. In my years of practicing veterinary medicine, this is only the third mesenteric torsion I have en-countered. Andrea's dog, who only last week I watched goofily toss her favorite toy around in the outdoor pen at our hospital, is not the dog that I want to encounter this morbidly fascinating condition in.

The surgical treatment for a mesenteric torsion is to untwist the guts into a straight line and then surgically excise the entire portion of the intestinal tract which has died. This leaves behind a short section of healthy intestines in the front, near the stomach, and a short section of intestines at the end nearest to the colon, which is then sewn back to-gether in the middle. Unlike a stomach torsion, this type of a torsion will result in a ninety-five percent death rate either during surgery or in the immediate post-operative period. Death rate not survival rate. Only five percent will live. Loser's odds for any sane gambler.

Andrea stands next to us in the surgery room observing the proceed-ings. She has blind faith that we will be able to help her dog. She works in a cutting-edge facility and she has faith in the exceptional skill of our surgeons. She believes Dr. Caldwell will be able to fix any surgical prob-lem that comes his way.

"That will need to be removed?" she questions us lightly about the blackened intestines that we have exteriorized.

Not a word has transpired between myself and the surgeon. There is nothing worth saying. We are both equally horrified at what we are see-ing and what we will now have to tell Andrea. We are both formulating the words in our head. Dr. Caldwell starts to speak. Without emotions he states the bleak statistics. He does not mince his words. "Five percent will live," he tells her. "Ninety-five percent will die. On the small chance that she does survive the surgery there will be an intense and prolonged postoperative period and if Autumn survives that she will now have short bowel syndrome. This means she cannot absorb nutri-ents properly and may have severe chronic diarrhea and a persistently emaciated body condition." He warns her that the bill may be double to triple what we expected. If she would like for him to proceed he will remove the deadened portion of the intestinal tract and he will sew the remaining healthy ends back together. If she would like to euthanize Autumn on the table at this moment, that would also be a fair option.

Andrea shakes her head. "Go ahead," she tells him, "give her the chance."

At her words I want to jump out of my sterile surgery gown and shake her gently and say, *Did you really, really hear what he just said? Let me explain it like this. With almost complete certainty Autumn is going to die. And when she dies it will be a slow and miserable death. And if she does not die, then you will forever after be cleaning up liquid diarrhea from your carpet, your chairs, and your furniture. Autumn will never again be the playful, bouncing, happy Boxer that you know. She will be sick and malnutritioned and have lifelong medical problems. All that and, alive or dead, this risky surgery is going to cost you a large amount of money. You will be paying this bill off for a very, very long time.*

I hold my tongue, it is not my place to say it and not my decision to make. I do not have a crystal ball which will accurately predict the outcome for Autumn. None of us do. Maybe Autumn will be one of the lucky five percent. Andrea has to make her own decisions, based on the information that we give her, and then she will have to live with the consequences of her decision.

Dr. Caldwell hurriedly starts to remove the blackened intestines. Based on how poorly she is doing under anesthesia he knows that surgery needs to be fast and efficient if he is going to get her off the operating table alive. And so he is. He ligates all of the blood vessels and then sews the two healthy remnants of intestines back together. In surgical terminology we call this an anastamoses. Autumn does survive the actual surgery. Andrea seems relieved. I'm still not sure she fully comprehends that the worst is yet to come, the post-operative period. Autumn's blood count has dropped precariously. She has lost seventy-five percent of her total blood volume in a matter of a few hours. We start blood transfusions. None of our valiant efforts help. Autumn dies three hours later with a total bill of about $4000. And, as I knew she would, she died a miserable death.

I wished again that Andrea had euthanized her on the table. I didn't want Andrea to watch her beloved pet die in this fashion. Andrea took a gamble that any sane poker player would never have touched. But this wasn't a card game, it was a life and death decision which revolved around a cherished member of her family. Andrea gambled, despite the pathetic odds, for the sole reason that her beloved friend, Autumn, was every bit worth that chance. And who am I to argue with that?

CHAPTER 18

MARTHA

Most of my adult life, and throughout my career as a veterinarian, I've owned cats. There are a few reasons for that. Partly it stems from the fact that I like to travel, either for long weekends or for extended trips, to exotic countries. Having a dog is not compatible with that lifestyle and, even more important, it is not fair to that animal. Cats are simpler. I love their warmth, their litheness, and their independent spirits. I love the way they look, curled up on a chair or next to the fireplace. I love how I can leave them for a night with a bowl of food and a clean litter box, and not have to worry. Dogs are fun to play with and to interact with during the course of my work day, but when I get home I don't want to walk them or feel guilt over my time away from them. For the most part I get my share of dogs all day long and I don't want animals persistently nuzzling me for attention when I return home.

On occasion I have chosen to take dogs home and that is usually because I do not see them as having another chance for adoption. These are the elderly dogs that have unexpectedly been lost, abandoned, or who belonged to a recently deceased person. They are the dogs who find themselves homeless and helpless in their frail elderly years. When most families go to adopt, they don't want to take on the responsibility of a pet that might soon die or who is likely to have a costly medical problem. These are the dogs that break my heart, the ones I tend to take into my home.

I walked into our ER room one night and strolled around to see what was admitted in the hospital that evening. In the far back corner I noticed a scraggly looking, grey-muzzled, but otherwise bright red Chihuahua circling the cage. Each time she arrived at the back wall, she caught a glimpse of her reflection in the aluminum cage panel and it would startle her. She would stop in her tracks, surprised at the sight of herself, and then turn and continue circling the cage, always to the left. She was finger painting tracks of feces around the floor of the cage as she went. Her left eye was proptosed, which means that it had been traumatically avulsed from the eye socket and was sticking out from her skull. It was an old injury that she must have been living with for some time, as the eye was crusted shut. On the other side of her face, a strand of pus was draining from an open wound beneath her only functioning eye. A draining tract in this location usually indicates an abscess of one of the upper molars, which erupts out through the skin below the eye. It would be hard to imagine more excruciating pain than what she was experiencing from the combination of her eye and her diseased tooth.

"Who's this?" I asked the floor technician.

"She was brought in as a stray yesterday," she said. "Be careful, she is as nasty as hell."

These words posed an immediate challenge to me. I love trying to soften a mean dog. Most of the time they're not really mean, they're just spoiled or used to getting their own way. I picked up the little filthy dog from the cage. She stiffened, and the most pronounced look of horror and fear formed on her face. Her lips curled up in a snarl. She was all too familiar with, and ready for confrontations. It was obvious that this elderly dog had spent her whole life fighting off humans. She was terrified and reacting with the only response that she knew – to attack any human who came near her. The dog visually stiffened and she then leaned away from me, with her little paws stiffened out in front of her, in an attempt to get her body as far away from me as possible. I tried to bring her close to my body in the hopes of feeling her body relax against mine. If you persist long enough, most animals will eventually give in to your embrace. It is one of the earliest things that you teach to a puppy. *When I hold you close to me you need to soften your body and stop struggling and then and only then will I let you go.* Most older animals will understand this as well if you are persistent.

Not this one. Any attempts to hold her close resulted in her becoming more frantic and blindly, repeatedly, and ineffectually snapping into the air in an attempt to bite me as hard as she could. I imagined that, with her bad eye and her diseased tooth, biting someone would really hurt but that didn't seem to deter her one bit. I continued this technique for a long time but this little dog would not come around. It wasn't hate, which the occasional dog emits, it was pure distrust, dislike and unwavering fear. When I put her on the ground, she would feebly charge at me with her mouth open, repetitively and viciously acting out the motions of ferocious biting. She would fearlessly stand her ground and, despite all my efforts to calm her, continue to put up her best fight. The technicians would periodically stand at the door and laugh heartily at the site of this elderly, partially blind, six pound ball of red fury charging and chasing their doctor around the room. Defeated, I put her away in a clean cage while I went to finish my work.

In the morning my conscience haunted me. I knew that she would be euthanized at the shelter. She was old and incorrigible. I wondered what time, and trust, and a loving home would do for this dog. I wondered what delivering her from the pain of her proptosed eye and her diseased teeth would do for her temperament. I wondered what a bad lot this dog had been given in her life. She seemed more mentally traumatized than any domesticated animal I had ever met. Since I had recently taken home one geriatric dog that needed attention, it seemed an appropriate time to bring in another. I named her Martha, after Martha Stewart. She needed a formidable name, as her tenacity had created respect in everyone that encountered her that night. The next day I took her to my day job and anesthetized her to fix her eye and her teeth. I removed almost 12 teeth from her mouth including her abscessed premolar. Her teeth were loose enough to fall out, and held in place only by the chunks of tartar that adhered her teeth to the bone. She must have been in an amazing amount of discomfort. I removed the proptosed eye which was bulging and ruptured. The chronic pressure must have felt like the worst migraine imaginable. I wondered what that amount of pain would do to the attitude of a person. If I had diseased teeth and an avulsed migraine of an eye, I would not be Little Miss Sunshine either. Martha woke up uneventfully, although somewhat confused. She seemed sedated and calm, and more comfortable than she had been in a very long time.

I created an imaginary story describing Martha's life. I imagined that she came from a large, poor family...a family with numerous children who didn't have time for her. Martha, like many Chihuahuas, was not an easy young dog. She was nippy, and got away with that behavior because people don't know how to deal with a nippy dog. Few seek out professional guidance to help with their biting dog. Her aggression probably escalated as she got older and as she became more confident in herself. She became a little dog who got what she wanted, when she wanted it. I'm sure this was exacerbated by the children who resorted to taunting her, pulling her hair or kicking her when she got near or acted out. Housed, but not loved, she fended for herself, eventually not caring to seek or receive any attention. Not cared for, not petted or brushed, and without any medical care provided, Martha became a nasty, isolated, lonely dog who never knew any bond with a human. I have met many poorly behaved dogs in my career and, as of this point, I had never before or since come across such a desperate, terrified, untrusting, unwanted dog. Martha tore at the strings that were attached to my heart and I wanted to try and help her. Help her to learn to trust a human and to learn that humans could be kind.

I brought Martha home and she transitioned into our quirky household uneventfully. Our disabled, deformed and ancient Italian Greyhound named Maude accepted this bizarre excuse of a dog quite willingly. They were both the same size, both geriatric, both had physical anomalies that were overtly laughable, and both had a spirit that one could not crush. They recognized that in each other immediately. Frail Maude quickly became the boss and Martha seemed content with that position. I marveled at how trusting Martha was with other dogs and cats, yet how untrusting she was of humans. Maude blossomed with Martha around. It was good for her to have someone to boss around and Martha seemed happy to finally have a compatriot and a friend.

For the first few months Martha remained untouchable. Any attempt to interact with her or lift her led her into a Tasmanian Devil-like frenzy of blind snapping and biting. We would carefully hold her up by her midsection with our arms extended in a spot where she couldn't quite turn and get us, but occasionally she managed to make contact with the few teeth she had left. Although my original intent was to try and adopt her to an elderly person who needed companionship, it soon became apparent by her unyielding behavior that Martha was going to be ours for the long run. I looked down at the half snarling, half smiling face glaring up at me and sighed. I just didn't have the heart to relocate this fragile, little soul to yet another new environment.

We had Martha for six more months before she died. It turned out to be six of the most rewarding months of my life. Little by little, Martha started to unassumingly accept us. She went about her new life in our home as if it was business as usual. She would march around our living room, always in a counterclockwise direction, and always clinging to the walls. After a few months, she showed her first signs of trust. When she circled around to where we were sitting on the couch, she would pause and lean her body against our legs. She would wait just long enough for us to stroke her back and then would continue on her circle around the room. She had finally learned that human touch could be nice, but it never stopped her from her habit of leaping and nipping into the air when we tried to leash her. But at least as time went on she put less and less energy into her efforts to get us. Unenthusiastically she would bite left and then bite right before giving it up. She still had the half snarl, half smile on her face but now with an expression that seemed to be saying *I know that you're trying to be nice to me so I'm trying hard not to bite you, but it is really, really hard to contain myself.*

Despite being partially blind and somewhat incoherent, Martha loved to march off and fearlessly explore our large yard. In whatever environment she was, she always circled to the left. I hoped this symptom was caused by the same head trauma which had dislodged her left eye but it soon became obvious that her neurological condition was progressing which made her disease more likely to be a brain disease or a brain tumor than head trauma. Head trauma would stabilize and might slowly improve, but it would not deteriorate.

Despite her slowly declining condition, Martha still gave the impression of having the time of her life. She thrived on being outdoors and was frighteningly unafraid to travel for long distances. She continued her methodical march that I had first observed back in the cage at the hospital. With her arms stiffly marching in front of her she looked like a militant wooly red soldier. She had a penchant for the water ditch which circled our property. Once Martha entered the ditch she would march from one end of it to the other, abruptly snapping around to the left in perfect form until she reached the covered pipes that were situated at the other end. She seemed content to march back and forth along the ditch's length for hours.

The ditch was a wonderful babysitter, as once she was immersed in it she seemed reluctant to leave its tight confining embrace. We were always happy to see the tip of her head moving around our lawn.

"Martha's in the ditch," we would pass the information to each other on our way out. It was our way of relaying that we knew her whereabouts and that she was safe and happy.

After six months of housing her, Martha got to the point where she would lean her body into us when we picked her up and would rest her head on our shoulders. It was another small step of trust in her loveless life. She seemed to really enjoy it. As her brain disease progressed, she became feebler and would spend longer periods of time pressed against us, seeming to want more and more of this newly found form of comfort. I never knew if she became nicer and more affectionate because of our loving care, or if it was because her brain tumor was worsening and obliterating out all of her hateful memories. In my heart I knew it was our love and not her disease but I could never scientifically prove that.

Due to her rapid decline into a semi-conscious state, I had to euthanize Martha on Christmas day. I refused to bring her to a hospital to do it. I wanted her last moments to be in the only kind place she had ever known. My boyfriend and I both cried as we sat with her on our laps during her last moments. I finally got the courage to push the pink euthanasia solution through her IV line. And then the most amazing thing happened when I started to do this. As I euthanized Martha, she started to endlessly wag her tail…a movement that we had never once observed in her during the whole time she had spent with us. Martha seemed to be saying "goodbye" and most of all "thank you."

She was saying, "Thank you for showing me love and a true home in the last months of my life."

CHAPTER 19

BOOBS

A loud commotion at the front reception area caught my attention. The noise came from a group of four teenage girls whose gestures and tone of voice relayed their agitation. The girls were taking turns peering into a box and then alternately talking into a cell phone which was being passed around the group. My triage technician went up to evaluate the contents of the box which turned out to be a three-month-old kitten.

"What happened?" asked my technician.

Guilty glances shot around the circle of girls.

"My boyfriend got mad and threw him into the wall," I overheard one of the girls mumble.

There was some shuffling and then a series of nervous giggling amongst the group. The group was escorted with the injured kitten, named Peter, into the exam room. When I arrived in the room, the girls were chatting lightly amongst themselves. In the ten minutes that it had taken to check the group into an exam room, the story about what had happened to Peter changed.

"He was accidentally dropped," girl number three explained to me.

Liar, I thought hiding my face so they wouldn't see my expression. It never fails to amaze me how rapidly stories change when people are trying to protect themselves.

"His arm's broken," offered girl number two, "that's why he's holding it out in front of him."

I peered into the box. A beautiful striped tabby kitten lay prone on the bottom of the box. His head was sprawled awkwardly backwards and his front feet extended stiffly in front of him. Looking closer at his eyes I noticed that his eyelids were swollen and his pupils were pinpoint. Over his left eye there was a small wound crusted with blood. Intermittently, Peter would make feeble attempts to move, but the best he could manage was pathetic circles as he pushed weakly with his left hind leg…the only functioning leg he had left.

"It's his left arm below the elbow," girl number four informed me.

I ignored her and continued my exam of Peter's head and neck.

"Right there," chimed in the same girl, insistently pointing to his left elbow.

Apparently these girls felt that I needed all the assistance I could get in determining what was wrong with their kitten. I went on with my exam. People are always trying to convince me of their own predetermined diagnoses.

"Thanks for your help girls, I'm sure I can figure this out on my own." Nervous giggling emerged from them.

I finished my examination of his spine and skull which, to me, was the obvious cause of his problems.

These girls badly wanted this to be a problem with Peter's leg. In their own minds, if it was his leg then it would be repairable. That way, they wouldn't have to face the fact that the kitten may be permanently disabled because their friend had violently slammed the tiny, helpless animal into a wall. If it was a broken leg, then it could be mended and girl number three would be able to return to her boyfriend in good conscience. Sadly, it wasn't his leg at all. Peter was suffering from a more permanent problem, one not so easily remedied – head trauma.

I studied them closer. They were four teenage girls with identical hairstyles, tight denim jeans, and all wearing clingy t-shirts with impressively low cut necklines. These voluptuous teenage girls were determined to display their goods to every young boy in the vicinity. Whichever way I turned in the small room, eight giant breasts with elongated cleavages confronted me at eye level.

"Its head trauma," I told them, taking care to speak clearly and look into their eyes. I guessed that they weren't really going to hear what I had to say.

"He's hemorrhaged into his brain and that's why he's unresponsive and unable to walk. His brain is damaged, which is why he is turning in circles and why his legs are stiffly extended in front of him."

I was trying not to mince my words. They needed to face the reality of Peter's injuries as well as the extreme intentional force that had been used to cause them.

"So it's not his leg?" numbers two and four gasped incredulously.

"No, I'm sorry it is not. It's a severe injury to his brain"

A group wail began. All four teenage girls' mouths instantaneously turned downwards. Almost in unison, dramatic tears welled out of their eyes. I wasn't quite sure why they needed my clinical assessment to bring out these emotions. The kitten had been twitching and semi-comatose for at least two hours now. Apparently no one in the group was capable of making an independent assessment without an authoritative figure to direct the course of their emotions. The group bawling became overwhelming and I left the room to give them a chance to compose themselves and to decide how they were going to help their kitten. When the grieving session had subsided I returned.

"What can we do for him?" asked number three. The group cranial waves were altering towards more productive thoughts.

These girls were collectively ignorant but I never doubted for a moment that they cared. The money for this office visit, which was probably taken from their monthly hair and nail fund allotment, was proof of their concern.

"Well ideally, if you are able, we would admit him to the hospital. If you are unable to do that, we can come up with another alternative which is not the ideal care. Hopefully it will work."

Even in the short time that Peter was here, I could see small signs of renewed consciousness in him. Young animals have an amazing resiliency and an uncanny ability to bounce back from injuries. Peter may not ever be the fully functional cat that he once would have been, but he may still be able to live a relatively normal life. The nice thing about animals with head trauma is that unlike humans they don't need to take an algebra test or thread a needle or write with a pen to succeed in life. Their only requirements are the fulfillment of basic life needs such as eating, drinking and playing.

"What do the fluids placed under his skin cost?" asked number one. She seemed to be the financier of the group.

"Twenty dollars," I replied

I have given out fluids to numerous animals per gratis in the past but I wasn't willing to do that for Peter. I wanted these girls to understand that there are consequences in life. This kitten was badly injured and there were emotional, physical and financial consequences to that. I was sad for these girls. Sad that they were associated with such a violent person and that they felt the need to protect him. I wanted to tell them that their friend's behavior was inexcusable. Over and over again, violence to animals has been associated with a propensity for violence to people.

I wanted to shock number three into reality and shout at her, "You might be next girlfriend. What will it be? A shove, a slap, a black eye or, maybe you'll 'accidentally' fall and end up in a coma too. Life's too short to hang out with assholes. Keep the good and send the bad right out that door. Bad influences are not helpful in your life."

Instead, I gave the fluids to Peter, instructed the girls on how to syringe feed him since he was barely swallowing, and sent them home to care for the maimed kitten. I hoped that he would live. I would report the incident to the local animal control officer as we were required to do, but I knew that, since Peter was alive, and since they had pursued medical care, it was unlikely that anything would be done. *I wish you the best young ladies*, I thought, as they departed en-bloc carrying semi-comatose Peter amongst them. *Stay united and take care of each other.* I sent telepathic thoughts after them in the hopes of influencing them to kick that violent friend out of their lives.

I formed a fantasy image of what I hoped would happen when they returned home. I envisioned the girls entering their home and confronting the boyfriend about his unacceptable behavior. They would surround him in a circle and as a group would yell wicked, teenage insults at him. They would then take turns pulling his hair and slapping him with their fake leather purses, while their barely-bound bosoms flopped precariously. And this time they would actually be angry enough to not care that they were messing up their beautifully coiffured hair.

It is not that uncommon for half-dressed people to show up at emergency hospitals. Pajamas, bathrobes, and slippers are attire that we see probably more frequently than any other business. Late one evening I was giving discharge instructions to a client in the lobby when a man rang the front doorbell. He seemed to be alone and I could not see any animals with him. It always worries me when a person shows up in the middle of the night without a visible pet in sight. Veterinary emergency hospitals which are open 24 hours and for previously described reasons are prime businesses to be robbed at gunpoint.

"We have a dog in the car who is bleeding. We can't stop the bleeding. Can you hurry?" the large man said to me with a disgusted tone that seemed to imply that I had taken too long to open the door.

"Okay," I said, wondering why this six-foot, two-inch man wanted me, a petite woman, to carry his dog inside for him. Also, if his dog was bleeding that badly, why wasn't he rushing in with it himself. Reluctantly, I started to follow him. Before I made it outside, a frazzled woman appeared carrying a 60-pound, muscular, brindle-colored pit bull whose leg was stained with blood. The woman collapsed on the floor as soon as she passed the door-well.

"He's bleeding, he's bleeding, he's' bleeding, Clyde's bleeding!" she screamed over and over again. "I don't want to lose him, I don't want him to die, he is all that I have."

She was lying on the floor huddled over her dog sobbing and quivering. She was a frail, thin young woman wearing men's boxer shorts, a low cut tank without a bra and no shoes. In this position her breasts were fully exposed under the scanty top. A swollen, pregnant belly stuck out from below the tank top. Her hair was stringy, mascara was dripping from her eyes, and she had numerous scabs all over her face. To complete this bizarre picture, a blood pressure cuff was tightly wrapped around her upper arm and the tubing was hanging down and dancing wildly as she quivered and sobbed. Her sobbing and choking was so intense that I was worried she might faint.

As an astute director and actor in my imaginary TV series, I knew immediately that it was that time again.

"Honey, honey," I said, putting my arm on hers trying to interrupt the frenzy of sobs, "let me look. Let me look and see what's wrong with Clyde."

She finally relaxed enough that I was able to maneuver poor shaken up Clyde out from under her grip. Soft brown eyes peered up at me worriedly from beneath the broad head as I examined him. Clyde had a small laceration on the bottom of his foot which had probably bled pretty badly at first but which had now clotted. The arteries on the underside of a paw are quite superficial and are easily lacerated by sharp objects. The extent of his injuries turned out to be a small wound and some dried blood on the bottom of his foot.

"He's okay," I told her softly, trying to calm the still sobbing woman.

"It's a small cut. We can fix it up. Let me bring him into the back, honey, and we'll make everything better."

The woman stopped crying, hugged Clyde tightly as if saying her final goodbyes, and then reluctantly let me have him. I was beginning to feel I deserved an Emmy for this role..

While his friend was uncontrollably sobbing on the floor, the man was standing in the corner inspecting the displays of coffee and tea. He was making no attempt to console her or even acknowledge her existence. *What a jerk,* I thought. Something was terribly wrong with this whole picture. The woman's reaction was way overboard for the situation, and this man's reactions were callous at best.

"I'm so sorry," the mascara-smeared, snotty-faced woman said, first looking down at her dangling exposed boobs and then up at me. "I am very emotional. I am pregnant," she told me, "I'm having twins."

The woman grabbed her breasts in both hands and lifted them up so that I could visualize them better. It seemed to be an awkward attempt to prove to me that she was properly equipped to handle two babies.

"I have a heart problem," she offered, pointing at her arm as an explanation for the blood pressure cuff that was dangling from her arm.

Her boyfriend continued to examine our Styrofoam coffee cups. I was now trying to understand why this large muscular guy would have allowed his pregnant girlfriend with a heart problem to carry the oversized dog into the hospital. I silently cursed him. *He's a really, really big jerk*, I decided.

A man and his child were checking out at the front desk. The man was trying to shield his child from the escalating peep show enfolding in front of us and the secretary was hurriedly attempting to check them out before anything crazier occurred. I took Clyde into the back of the hospital. Clyde seemed relieved to get away from his hysterical mother and was vigorously pulling me towards the back of the hospital. That was a change, an animal who actually wanted to go to the back of a veterinary hospital. From his perspective, the prep room of a busy ER hospital must be an extremely peaceful place to be, compared to being in the presence of his mother.

"She's tweaking," said Kim, the front desk receptionist, as I passed her. She was referring to our shared belief that these two must be on some type of drugs.

Fatally hemorrhaging, Clyde was enjoying the attention he was receiving from my technicians in the back and we easily fixed his laceration with a few sutures and a bandage. I returned to the room where Kim had placed his owners. Recognizing the need to remove them from the reception area as quickly as possible, she had moved them into an exam room. Scenes like that in the waiting room are not good for business. The woman seemed calmer now and the boyfriend was actually choosing to answer when I spoke to him.

I noticed that my exam room was now decorated with a large assortment of movie-sized boxes of candy. Ceremoniously spread throughout the room, on the counters, and exam table, were boxes of Reese's pieces, Almond Joys, Malted Milk Balls, and Milky Ways. There were mascara-smeared, wet tissues crumpled up and distributed amongst the boxes. The man, who was indulging from each of the boxes, periodically turned and placed a candy into the mouth of the woman. I tried to ignore the odd feast of chocolate that was ensuing in front of me as I explained the discharge instructions to them.

I dragged the reluctant Clyde back into the room. He didn't want to return to them any more than I did. With a mouth packed full of choc olate, the woman explained how the injury had occurred. "He jumped through the screen window trying to come after me when I left the house. I don't understand why he's such a nervous dog."

"I don't understand either," I replied resignedly, as I stared at this cracked-out woman's swollen belly which contained two unborn children.

Actually, I did understand but I didn't think that sharing my opinion would be helpful. *Clyde is neurotic because you are neurotic. Your neurosis is compounded because you have chosen to solve your problems through the use of drugs and men who are not healthy for you. Not only have you passed on your neuroses and insecurities and failings to your dog, but most likely you will do the same to your beautiful twins that are about to be born.* But I didn't do it. Instead, I shut out my personal thoughts and helped her to the lobby with Clyde.

The couple paid us with a tall stack of crumpled bills that she pulled from her disheveled purse.

"Payday," she explained when she noticed the questioning face of the secretary. "I need to get to the bank to deposit it."

We both reflected on what kind of business would pay in a stack of five and ten dollar bills, but once again we silently kept our opinions to ourselves. You learn quickly, as a professional of any vocation, that keeping your opinion to yourself is a more diplomatic approach.

One client brought in his beautiful Brittany Spaniel so I could examine a spot on its belly. "My dog has a tick and I can't get it off. I think its head is buried under the skin."

Many owners are fixated with the belief that a tick's head is still buried under the skin of their dog after they have removed it. Most people have ticks so demonized that they convince themselves that the creature must still be living in their pet long after they have flushed it down the toilet. The medical truth is that when you are trying to pull a tick off of your pet, the tick will hang onto its own head with gusto. They are no more willing to dislocate their head from their body then you or I are. What people commonly believe is a tick's head, is usually a small inflammatory swelling which is left behind, caused by the injection of the tick's saliva under the skin.

I examined the site in question. There was a bright red, raisin-shaped structure on the dog's belly. Patches was sensitive about the structure and seemed extremely reluctant to let me touch it. I inspected it and looked up at the man a bit incredulously.

"That's not a tick, that's his nipple," I told him. I diplomatically left out that, at this point, it was a very swollen, red and irritated nipple.

"I've been trying to pull it off all morning," he informed me.

"Well stop that," I replied, speaking slowly and with emphasis. "It is not coming off any time soon."

I had a new appreciation for how kind and patient a dog Patches was.

"He doesn't have nipples, he's a male dog," the man continued in defense of himself.

I looked at him again. *That's it, my job as an educator ends here.* I did not have it in me to point out that he was a man and that I was pretty sure that if he looked under his own shirt, he would find that he too had nipples. This one he was going to have to figure out for himself.

CHAPTER 20

...AND BUTTS

"**R**ect 'em, damn near killed 'em," my first boss used to yell out loudly whenever I inadvertently forgot this annoying ritual of his and used the word 'rectum' in his presence. He thought himself quite funny and liked to insert the word rectum into his sentences in place of words that he thought sounded similar.

The words rectum and anus are two different words that are used to describe the same anatomical body part. They may be words that are rarely used in most business settings, but their use is a fairly common occurrence in the veterinary world. Rectal irritations, rectal masses, prolapsed rectums, anal glands, and anal abscesses are examples of some of the terms that come up regularly in our vocabulary.

In a routine appointment, the owners must think that we're obsessed with their pet's rectums. For accuracy most temperatures are taken that way, and we're often seen doing rectal exams either to express their pet's anal glands or to better evaluate the pet's health. Owners seem mystified as to why we see the need to stick our finger up the butts of their pets. It is most certainly not for our own personal amusement. I am checking to see if there are any enlarged lymph nodes, or tumors in the colon, or to see if the animal's pelvis is broken. We can also feel if there are sticks or rocks passing through their colon, or if the surface of the colon feels bumpy or unusual in any way. In horses and cows, a rectal exam is a way to tell if they are pregnant, or a way to evaluate the adjacent organs, or to see if we can feel a twist or a mass in the intestines. So, in short, there are a multitude of legitimate reasons for veterinarians to have our fingers up your pet's bottom.

When I was in high school, I went to observe a veterinarian working in her office. At her first appointment, the owner requested that the vet express her dog's anal sacs. Anal sacs are two structures on either side of the rectum which contain fluid meant to scent the feces. I am convinced that their only real function is to annoy veterinarians. The vet that I was spending the day with was tiny, about five feet tall, just at eye level with the dog's rectum. When she expressed his anal glands, she received a direct bulls-eye squirt of anal gland material to her left eye.

"Oh, I hate when that happens," she cried out wiping the sticky, thick material off of her face.

At the time, it was the most disgusting thing I had ever seen. I was sure that I would have a few more choice words and expletives than that if that ever happened to me. I think that most high school students, after having witnessed an event like that, would have left the room immediately, returned to their guidance counselor's office, and changed to a less messy future career such as optometry. Not me, anal glands in the face or not, I was deeply committed to my goal of becoming a veterinarian.

As a prospective veterinarian you gather information about the field as quickly as you can to avoid repeat occurrences in the future. One lesson that I learned early on in my career was that I needed to be very careful with my choice of words. I was working with a Labrador who was brought to our hospital because he was scooting his bottom along the ground. The owner was a handsome, young lawyer. I was young and I was single. I suspected that the front desk ladies, who liked to play matchmaker, had intentionally scheduled him in on my appointment slot.

"Has your dog ever had problems with his anal sacs?" I asked nonchalantly.

Anal gland impactions are the most common culprit for a dog to be scooting. I was mentally formulating a short list of what else could be causing his dog's scooting if anal sacs were not the issue. The room became suddenly quiet. I could see the owner's expression change and then his face turn slowly red. His reply was slow as he seemed to be composing his words. I wasn't entirely sure of what had upset him, until he replied very clearly and very indignantly, and in a most lawyerly voice, "MY DOG DOES NOT HAVE ANAL SEX."

He gathered up his belongings and stomped out of the room, dragging his dog behind him. Left alone in the room, I felt my own face start to turn red and then from somewhere deep in my belly, an uncontrollable giggle emerged. That was the last time that would ever happen. I vowed that, from here on forward, I would refer to the structures that are present within a dog's rectum as anal glands, and never again use the term, 'anal sacs.'

Even after all these years, it still makes me uncomfortable when I have to reach for the glove and ask the owner to turn their pet around so their pet's backside is facing me.

"I don't like this any more than you do," I tell the pet in a truthful apology before attempting entry into his butt. If given the choice, I prefer to perform rectal exams in the back room away from the incriminating eyes of the owners.

As much as we hate doing them, they are an extremely important part of a thorough physical exam. On a golden retriever belonging to one of my favorite clients, I failed to do a rectal exam on his yearly visit. As a result of that lapse, I missed finding a tumor in his colon. A few months later, we found large nodules in Tucker's lungs which had metastasized from that colonic tumor. I had a hard time looking that owner in the eye. I knew that I had failed to find that mass at his last exam because I had failed to do a rectal exam on his annual health visit.

Sometimes when I am examining a pet, people will show me the little white rice granules which are stuck to their pet's anus.

"We don't feed him rice. I don't know where he's finding food with rice in it," they tell me.

I take the rice-like kernel that they show me and place it on a slide so they can look at it more closely. There they can then see that the segment is wriggling and alive.

"Those are tapeworm segments. They are pieces of a worm that your pet gets from ingesting mice or fleas," I inform them, speaking in my most neutral doctor voice because I know that they are about to have a strong guttural reaction to what I am saying. "And the reason they're rubbing their butts on your floor is that it makes their anus itchy, and they are trying to dislodge the worm segments."

I don't add that the segments are probably dispersed throughout their beautiful home and imbedded into the fibers of their nice living room carpet. I watch the owners' faces for the horrified expression that I know will soon arrive when the realization of what I have just said hits home.

"The good news is that they are very easy to get rid of." I smile and hand them a little white pill to give to their dog. Owners love giving pills especially when it is a quick solution to such a disconcerting problem.

I remember well the first day that I nervously went to the emergency and referral hospital where I work to interview with the man who might soon be my new boss. I was directed over to one of the wet sinks where he was standing with a lifeless cat. He had just finished euthanizing this stray cat because its injuries had proven to be life threatening and were too extensive to reasonably treat. We were standing across the sink from each other discussing some of the duties that the ER position entailed. It was a few minutes into the conversation before I realized he was doing a rectal exam on the dead cat while he was speaking to me. As odd as this seems, I knew exactly why he was doing it. Like the good surgeon that he was, he was evaluating the extent of the cat's pelvic fractures. For him, the dead cat provided a learning opportunity to help diagnose the next animal who might arrive with similar pelvic fractures. I didn't comment on what he was doing but the oddity of the situation didn't escape me. I was standing next to my handsome, successful, highly skilled future employer, who was nonchalantly interviewing me with his finger up the ass of a dead cat. Suddenly my potentially future boss didn't seem so intimidating. This was better than the old trick of making yourself more comfortable by imagining a person in his underwear. *What a bizarre profession this is*, I reflected for the hundredth time in my career as I returned his inquiries. I was as equally capable as he of pretending that a rectal exam on a dead cat during an interview is an ordinary occurrence in business.

People take their pet's butt problems very seriously. In veterinary school, a dog came in whom we dubbed 'Mick' because he had upper and lower anal flaps that protruded and flapped as he moved. From the back view, his rectum resembled Mick Jagger's lips. The internal medicine specialist did a variety of hormone tests to determine the cause of this embarrassingly prominent anus, but to no avail. Much to the owner's consternation, there was no medical treatment for poor Mick's embarrassing condition. Mick was going to have to continue on with his doggy life, sporting ridiculously large anus lips which would flap behind him. I don't really think the dog was overly concerned about his anal problem, but apparently it was a problem for the owners. They were embarrassed enough about the appearance of their dogs unsightly anus, to spend several hundred dollars in an attempt to fix the protruding appendage. Woefully, modern medicine cannot fix everything.

In reality, anuses and butts are no laughing matter. Butt function is critical to an animal's existence. Few people will tolerate an animal that is incontinent. My heart goes out to the poor cat who comes in with a tail-pull injury so severe that its tail has been dislocated from its body. This type of injury can occur if they get it caught on a fence while jumping over it, but sometimes it happens when a kid thinks it is funny to swing the cat around and around in a circle while holding on to its tail. When the tail is pulled from the body it can tear the nerves that innervate the colon so they can lose all ability to retain feces. When I see the cat come in with an anus gaping open so wide that I am able to view the contents of its colon, I know that this kitty is in big trouble.

Incontinence happens to older dogs but for a different etiology. These guys have severe arthritis of their spines. In this case, the nerves that emerge from the spinal cord and sensitize the colon, are pinched so severely that the dog becomes incontinent, causing it to leak urine or drop feces around the house. Sadly these geriatric dogs are also doomed. Owners will put up with this for a while in their elderly pet but will arrive in tears at the veterinary hospital when it becomes the last straw in a growing list of medical problems.

Butt problems abound even on emergency duty. One night a woman arrived to the ER hospital because her dog was incessantly scooting and chewing at his rear. Anal glands are the most common cause of this symptom. On close examination of his rear end, I was surprised to find that this time there was a different culprit. I thought I had seen it all, but apparently not.

"Do you do any sewing?" I asked.

She looked at me puzzled, wondering what sewing had to do with her dog dragging his butt around her home.

"Well I do have a sewing room. I haven't had any projects recently but Jasmine does go in there from time to time."

"Well, Jasmine has a needle piercing through her rectum which is holding it together in a tight little pucker." (Well, I didn't actually say the part about the tight pucker but it's funny.) There was silence for a moment and then we both broke out laughing. Jasmine who was scooting uncomfortably around the exam room didn't think the situation was funny at all. We sedated Jasmine and the offending needle was removed from her rectum with care. She woke up from the sedative and bounced gleefully around the room, thrilled to finally be free of the constricting pain that had afflicted her poor rectum for the last few hours.

Even snakes have rectal problems. But in snakes it is not actually called a rectum. It's called a cloaca. Once a Burmese Python showed up at my ER with a cloacal prolapse. I have seen many rectal prolapses in dogs and cats, but this would be my first cloacal prolapse. Snakes will forever frighten me. I have a real phobia of the creatures, and this phobia developed long, long before the mamba incident. But that incident didn't help my fears. Despite knowing all of the medical and behavioral facts about snakes, I have always been convinced that they really are slimy and icy cold to the touch.

I examined my tubular patient. *Patients should not be tubular in shape* I thought to myself, *they should be rounder with appendages called arms and legs emerging from them.* I noted a red tissue swelling protruded from the snake's cloaca. *And rectum is so much nicer sounding than cloacas.*

I was lucky that evening that our expert herpetologist technician, Sean, was on shift and happy to restrain the biblically evil serpent.

"You hold the front end and I'll work on the back end," I hissed through clamped teeth. "Hold it tight and don't let me see its head."

Sean was happy to oblige, mostly because he didn't want his ER doctor fainting so early in the evening.

I will do my job as needed, as the situation arises, but not without a certain amount of whining, especially when snakes are involved. We anesthetized the snake. I lubricated the exposed tissue and then I pushed and prodded until the prolapsed tissue disappeared back into the snake's cloaca in the position where it belonged. I placed sutures around the cloaca opening to maintain the replaced swollen tissue in place. The sutures would be removed in one week, which is about when the snake would need to eat and defecate again. I pondered how one could feel affection for a creature who is so metabolically slow that it only needed to eat once a month..

"Let's put her in some water," Sean said, "this will calm her and help her muscles relax so that the prolapse will stay in its place."

I thought putting the snake into a fail-safe container was a great idea. I was sure that behind those beady eyes, it was plotting to methodically hunt me down, constrict me, and then swallow me whole as revenge for having just having sewn its anus closed.

"You do whatever you need to do for it, just don't ever make me work on the rectum of a butt-less animal again," I replied, placing strong emphasis on my words to make sure that he clearly understood that I was serious. In afterthought I should have been more specific and stated "buttless, tubular animals".

CHAPTER 21

GANGSTERS AND CREEPS

Veterinary medicine is an emotionally charged business. Emotions emerge from owners in a wide variety of forms. Some of them appear paralyzed with fear, some are paralyzed with grief, some of them yell, some use expletives, and some resort to threats when they are frightened for their pet. On rare occasions they resort to physical intimidation. I remember one incident where a man, who was unhappy with the costs of an emergency surgery, threatened to break one of our veterinarian's hands if his pet wasn't brought to surgery immediately. The surgeon's response was that the end result of that threat would be unlikely to result in a hastening of the procedure that needed to be done for his dog.

At least the loud vocal complainers are placing their frustrations out front on the table rather than leaving us guessing about how they feel about the situation. With time and effective communication they usually quiet down and discuss the situation rationally. It is the other type of client that is more worrisome to me...the ones you know are upset, but just silently simmer as you pass their pet back over to them. With that type of person, I find myself wondering if I am going to receive an angry letter in the near future or, even worse, a letter from their lawyer or the veterinary board.

One memorable encounter I had with a client was a very different form of intimidation from anything that I had ever experienced before that point. This client scared me at a very visceral level. The man was middle aged, heavy set, and with a dark complexion. He wore shaded glasses and a waist length wool jacket. He carried his small dog into our hospital and explained that he had accidentally shot her while target practicing with friends. He told me that his dog had intermittently run behind the target while he was shooting. I didn't bother to ask the obvious question of why he hadn't tied his dog up after she ran behind it the first time. I assumed that either he was already aware of the stupidity of his actions, or that he figured he was that good of a shot.

The little dog lay on the table on her side breathing heavily. She could sit up for short periods, but then would collapse down with a distressed look. I identified a bullet hole that had entered into her abdomen. I could not identify the exit hole. The dog seemed more stable than I expected, considering the type of injury, but I also knew that if the bullet had damaged some vital organs, her condition would rapidly take a turn south in the upcoming hours. I was concerned that there might be a slow internal bleed or a ruptured intestine.

Usually when people have inflicted an injury on their pet, they will bend over backwards to remedy the situation regardless of the cost. This is a reflection of their feelings of guilt. Not in this case

"Molly sustained a bullet injury to her abdomen," I told the man. "This is what we need to do to try and help her."

I went on to outline the treatment that we would need. After explaining the medical and probable surgical care necessary to save his dogs life, I had my technician present him with an estimate of the cost. Up until this time the man had been quietly agreeable. I presumed he was feeling guilt over what he had done to his dog.

"He wants to speak to you," my technician said, exiting the room. "He's interesting," she added as an afterthought.

I went back in the room. The man was standing at the far end of the room with his back to me. He was staring out the window.

"You are sure my dog needs all of this?" he inquired.

I assured him that most definitely she did.

"I'm not paying that," he said softly, without turning around.

"Okay," I replied, recalculating in my head how we could help his bullet shredded dog. I was surprised that he was bargaining, considering the cause and the extent of his dog's injury. I then discussed alternative but less viable treatment options for Molly.

"We do have financing programs to offer," I went on, still misconstruing what he was saying.

"You don't understand," he went on speaking with his back to me. I wondered what it was that was fascinating him so much out there. "You will go ahead and do what is necessary to treat my dog, but I am not going to pay that. I am not paying anything."

I laughed silently to myself, careful not to let any sound emerge. Who was this guy kidding? He had stupidly injured his own dog and he wanted us to pay for his dog's expensive tests, treatment, and possible surgery. The man continued on dictating to me, in a cold monotone voice, the medical treatment that he expected for his dog, never once bothering to turn around to meet my eye. I felt the hairs on my neck rise. I had the distinct impression of speaking to someone who was aware that he had deadly authority...kind of like a Mafia Don you hear about on the news. He was still wearing his coat in the warm room. I wondered if he had something concealed beneath it. Scenes from 'The Godfather' flashed in my mind.

I've had many a client indirectly try to get out of paying a bill or flatly tell me that the pet's care was not affordable to them, but this was most interesting because it was the first time someone had just demanded my services for nothing. This was also a much more intimidating manner than being directly confronted. I started to realize how strange this man's thinking was and also that we were alone in the building with him. I swallowed hard and forced myself to reply to him exactly how I would reply to any other client.

I kept my voice soft and even toned as I said, "Well we can just send Molly home on pain medications and antibiotics and hope that the bullet hasn't hit anything vital." I offered to have the medications made up.

He continued to avoid my gaze.

"The medications are on you," he stated quietly, authoritatively. "You will give me the medications."

I decided that this man was delusional. Maybe HE had watched too many gangster movies. This was the tame Northwest, not the streets of Chicago in the 1920's. Mafia or not, now I was angry. I was not going to be intimidated by this man. *Get some kahunas, get some kahunas,* I chanted to myself in an attempt to gain courage for what I was about to say next.

"No," I stated in my most confident voice, "no, I will not give you the medications for free. This is your dog, who you shot, and you will pay for the services and medicines dispensed like everybody else who walks through these doors. If you do not want to pay or don't want our services then you will leave the building with your pet and take her home where most likely she will die of her injuries."

In slow motion the man turned toward me for the first time. I braced myself for whatever was about to occur next. My professional side told me it would be a verbal assault but my imagination was ready for the gun fight. He stopped and surveyed me silently. I watched his hands to see if they would reach inside his jacket. They never did. Instead, he strode toward the exam table, sending me furtively backing up. He wordlessly picked up his writhing dog, stalked across the lobby, and exited the building.

Relieved, I peered out the window after him to see if he had a low riding antique car, with a Fedora-wearing driver ready at the wheel for a quick departure. Contrary to my active imagination, all I saw was a dirt smeared Ford pick-up leaving the parking lot. I never did hear what happened to poor Molly. In some ways, I didn't want to know what had happened to Molly because I never wanted to have another encounter of any type with Don Capone's nephew again. For a month after the event, each time that I turned my cars ignition key, I silently prayed that it was not rigged with explosives. I also had vivid nightmares of finding my horse's head tucked under my bed covers.

You expect your work environment to be safe and protected. It is always a surprise to me when something happens to break the sanctity of that space. Creepy people are everywhere.

One early morning, at the end of a busy shift, I was asked to euthanize a rabbit for an elderly gentleman. He told us the bunny was failing rapidly. The sweet, grey-haired man was sitting in the room hugging 'Bobby' to his chest. I explained the euthanasia process to him while tears streamed down his face. He hugged Bobby tightly to his body.

"It's okay Doc, I'm used to this kind of thing," the gentleman told me. "Go ahead."

I always find euthanizing the pets of elderly people the most difficult task. Often they are alone and have few other things to look forward to in their lives. For many of them, their pets are what keep them getting up each morning.

I quietly helped Bobby out of this life and leaned over towards the man to confirm, with my stethoscope, that Bobby was gone. The tearful gentleman put both of his hands on my forearm as I was doing so.

"He's gone. I am so sorry," I told him, truly feeling badly for this man who obviously loved his bunny so much. I reflected on how odd of a companion a bunny is for a geriatric person. I walked over to the exam table to make notes in the record.

The man got up, wiped his eyes, and crossed the room to throw away his tissues. As he passed me in the moderately spaced exam room, he placed his hands on my shoulders and slid closely by me on his way to the bin. He really didn't need to be that close to me, but I also know that people are often looking for comforting touches at such an emotional time.

I took Bobby's body into the back and ceremoniously placed him in a blanket-lined coffin box which we use for such occasions. I then solemnly transferred Bobby into the man's waiting hands. He was still wiping away the tears and my heart went out to him.

"Thank you," he said to me. "Let me give you a hug. I need a hug"

This poor man. He put Bobby down and then put his arms around me and hugged me closely, squashing me into his chest. After what seemed like more than an appropriate amount of time, I started to pull away. The contact was starting to feel awkward. In the process of extracting myself, I distinctly felt his hand land firmly around the bottom of my right breast, giving it a tight squeeze, and I could sense his other hand groping for my left one. I pulled away with significantly more force this time, and willfully pushed his resisting hand off of my right boob. I was shocked and taken aback and not quite sure of how to respond to such a moment. I was still trying to confirm in my head what had just happened, when he grabbed the box containing Bobby's body and rushed out the door.

My mouth was agape and I had a sordid feeling of just having been violated. It was a short moment and not the worst of offenses, but still it was an unexpected assault at five in the morning. It was shocking to me that this had just occurred in my place of business when I was wrapped up in the emotions and somberness of euthanizing a person's beloved pet. My feelings for the guy shifted one hundred and eighty degrees.

"What a nasty, dirty, disgusting old man," I vented loudly to my technicians as I exited the room. "I cannot believe he had the gall to do that." They were equally as disgusted as I, when they heard what had happened.

I reflected on what a person could be thinking who would schedule an appointment to euthanize his animal, and then cop a feel on the way out. He was either extremely lonely or extremely sick. Our secretary, on hearing about the disturbing encounter, waved her hands in a circular fashion at her own ample bosom and announced that if he ever comes in again, I should proclaim in a loud voice to him that, "THESE ARE NOT BUNNIES!"

And then for just the briefest of moments, our troubled mood was washed away by our laughter.

CHAPTER 22

HISTORICALLY SPEAKING

Our patients can't speak to us, so veterinarians rely heavily on the owner's history, and a good physical exam to figure out what is wrong. The truth for every aspiring young veterinarian out there is that a large number of your cases can be solved with just these two components. There is no diagnostic test or sophisticated imaging technique that can supercede what you find out from a history and thorough exam. Unfortunately, obtaining histories can sometimes be an amusingly frustrating endeavor.

I try to question people in a specific, concise manner in order get pertinent medical information from them. In return, I am hoping for specific, concise answers that are given in a timely fashion. The responses I get the majority of the time, are neither short winded or pertinent. When trying to determine how long their dog has had trouble breathing, I usually get responses explaining how the dog's sibling died of cancer, how he was the runt of the litter, or I learn how much their other dog loves to swim. *HOW LONG,* I want to repeat slowly and with emphasis. This particular question requires a quick, two-syllable answer only. If I ask *WHAT* their pet has vomited, I may get told every brand

187

name of food they've eaten since they were two, and how their other dog had a virus which caused bad diarrhea when it was a puppy. Not easily deterred, I will continue to persevere and gently ask the question in a variety of manners until I get the appropriate response to the question that I am asking. In theory, our ability to effectively communicate and draw out the correct information from our clients should improve as we develop in our careers. This is not always the case.

One Sunday, Dr. Burns was working on a critical patient who had just arrived and he asked me to go into the exam room to get a quick history from the owners so he could better figure out why this animal was so ill. The dog seemed to be dying, and he needed fast answers about what had happened, to help him treat the dog appropriately. Easier said than done, it seems. After speaking to the owners for what seemed like an eternity, I returned to my colleague to relay what they had told me. The dog appeared lifeless, and the silence in the room told me that things were not looking hopeful for this pup.

"Well the owners told me that he collapsed once on the stairs. This happened about thirty minutes after they had eaten pizza for dinner. Then he collapsed once in the hallway leading into the living room, on a wood parquet floor that they just waxed and which they believed was quite slippery, and then again in the kitchen near the sink. They recently refinished their kitchen and he is afraid of their tile floor. He also ate a piece of their chicken sandwich last week, he wakes his owners up every night at 4:00 a.m. to go potty, and he loves to play with balls, specifically tennis balls."

I repeated to him, verbatim, what the owners had just told me in the room. The owners had just wasted valuable time, when seconds counted toward helping their dog. My colleague gave me a harrowed, yet sympathetic look. He knew exactly how I felt. He too had experienced the frustrations of an owner's prolonged and useless history many times in his career.

"It is amazing what people focus on at critical times isn't it?" he said with a conciliatory nod, while continuing last chest compressions on the dog who had long since died.

Some of the histories that I get will give me small insight into the owner's lives that I am not sure I really want to know. One morning, a nervous looking woman brought her cat in to see me with the complaint that his back was hurting. My exam confirmed that she was right and that the cat truly was hypersensitive to having his spine touched. I started to mull over all of the possible causes of spinal pain in cats.

The woman leaned toward me, nervously wringing her hands and whispered conspiratorially, "I think it's my ex-husband's fault. He's a drug addict, and I think that he has been sneaking into my home at night and injecting my cat in the back with methamphetamines."

Here we go again. Does this stuff happen anywhere else? *Someone please tell me if I am secretly being filmed for a soap opera.*

I tried hard not to laugh. I may not be the brightest veterinarian out there, but the one thing I am sure of is that no cat is going to passively sit there while somebody shoves a needle full of stimulants into his back. It's hard enough for us, as trained professionals, to give a cat a shot unaided without risking losing our fingers. I had to give her credit that it was one potential diagnoses that I had not considered. A good veterinarian's job is to come up with a list of possible diagnostics that may be the cause of an animal's medical problem, and then try to eliminate the list one by one. This list of possible causes are called differential diagnoses and are listed under the abbreviation ddx in medical records. The 'junkie ex-husband shooting its cat up with speed for fun syndrome' was not listed under the heading of spinal pain in any of the veterinary textbooks that I had ever read. I looked closer at the frail, nervous-looking woman. I had a new perspective about what happened behind closed doors at her house.

"I guess that's one consideration," I replied, trying to give some validation to her suspicions. "But why don't we get some x-rays of Tommy and see what else we can find. If we find something on x-rays, then at least we can eliminate your ex-husband as the cause of his pain and then you won't have to worry about him anymore."

I congratulated myself for once again ending tonight's episode with a very plausible and comforting scene that the audience would appreciate.

If my daily story is not a soap opera, then it may be a very odd reality show that is being filmed. I sure hope not, because this actually IS my real life. But still, I can't help wondering because bizarre events seem to happen all too frequently on my emergency shifts. One night, contrary to my wishes for a boring evening, the series played out as follows. A beautiful, well-dressed couple showed up in the wee hours of the morning. The woman was tall and lanky with platinum white dyed hair, tight jeans, and an elegant blouse. I was immediately envious of her gorgeous silky face and sleek figure. Speaking in a strong Swedish accent, in the staccato manner that Nordic people have, she explained that her beloved cat, 'Poofy,' was falling over and not acting right.

"She wouldn't eat tonight, this she has never before done," she told me.

The man with her was also Swedish, also with platinum dyed hair, but his was spiked. He too was immaculately dressed, wearing pleated trousers with suspenders, and a starched blue shirt with diamond cufflinks. I couldn't stop staring at them. *Where do these people come from,* I wondered. Located in the middle of a small, backwards city, I was speaking to a stunning overdressed Swedish couple in the wee hours of the morning about their elderly cat named Poofy of all things. They seemed like the perfect movie star couple. They were perfect looking, perfectly dressed, probably rich, and of course madly in love.

From my examination, it was obvious to me that Poofy was profoundly anemic and weak from lack of blood and oxygen being delivered to her tissues. I ran a quick test to measure the degree of her anemia. It was 11 percent, normal being 40. This meant that she was missing 75 percent of the red blood cells in her bloodstream. I told the couple that in order for Poofy to live, she needed a transfusion. That alone would cost about $400. That was just the beginning, as we needed diagnostics to determine what was wrong with her, and then she would need to be hospitalized and treated. Before we could start treatment, they needed to understand that, given the seriousness of her disease, even with all of the most advanced medical care I could offer or an unlimited budget, her disease may still prove to be fatal.

After a long period of agonizing, the couple painfully told me that they could not treat Poofy.

"Our lives are all messed up," the well-groomed, beautiful man told me. "We are in the process of separating and we don't have the time or the ability to provide consistent care for her".

I was stunned, first by the news that this perfect couple could possibly be "messed up" and, second, by the smashing of my illusion and that they could be unhappy and leaving each other. It all sounds silly in retrospect, but this was the romantic fantasy that I had playing in my head that would work to also offer the necessary romantic thread to my reality series. I wondered why they were choosing to share this aspect of their lives with me, as I didn't need any of that information to properly treat Poofy.

I looked at the couple somewhat differently now. It wasn't the seamless couple that I had imagined twenty minutes before. They were young, fragmented, and barely hanging on. The loss of Poofy might be one of the last events that they shared together. I relayed the euthanasia process and the choices of cremation for Poofy.

"Can I have her ashes returned?" The silky women snuggled up to her soon-to-not-be husband, her means of inquiring if he would pay for the extra cost involved in a private cremation.

"Of course," he offered, in what seemed to be a final conciliatory gesture as he handed over his credit card.

I left the room to tell my technicians, who were in the back holding Poofy, of the couple's decision. Before I returned, I peeked in through the peephole to insure that I was not disturbing a private moment. The beautiful couple were entwined in a silent hug of extreme grief. She had her face pressed into his neck as he rifled his hand through her silky platinum hair. For that brief moment in time their relationship wasn't shattered. They WERE the fantasy couple that I imagined in my head. United, happy and of course in love.

Another beautiful ending to my show.

CHAPTER 23

YOUR CHOICE

"**N**ow this is how it's going to work. You stand there and you shut up. And when I'm done talking, and only when I am done, then you may speak. I am going to let you know exactly how you are going to proceed with my cat's care."

The man speaking these words was standing across the exam table from me, on my emergency shift, in exam room number four. His wife was sitting at his side, nodding her head at each word that he spoke. His words were the response that I got after I explained to him that his cat was in critical condition because it was not able to urinate. It was unable to urinate because there was a stone lodged in its urethra. If the urinary obstruction was not relieved this evening, his cat would die before morning. His choices were down to two: he could treat it, or he could euthanize it.

This man was not happy with my recommendations for hospitalized care. When the technician presented him with the written estimate for the care that his cat needed, he responded by crumpling up the paper and throwing it against the wall. This was followed by the verbal tirade that I was now listening to when I went back in to speak to him. My intent was to try and discuss other options that might be feasible for him. But after sitting through his rant, I knew that rational discussion was not going to happen. Silently I cautioned myself not to over react to his words. Don't feed into his anger, stay calm, be professional.

That's fine, mister, speak all you want, I'll just shut up, as you requested, and listen.

I silently let him finish. It always puzzles me as to why people pay an expensive emergency exam fee, presumably to get an expert opinion, and then insist on telling me what they think is wrong and how they think it should be treated. If this man did not want to hear what I had to say, then I wasn't going to argue with him.

He did end up leaving the cat but only after leaving specific instructions on what we could and could not do. His requests were not the ideal medical care, but at least it would give the cat a fighting chance. I hoped, for the cat's sake, that this would work. I tried to explain the negatives to the treatment plan that he had dictated, but he interjected each time that I spoke.

"I would have kicked his ass out onto the sidewalk right then and there," a colleague of mine said when I told her what happened a few days later. "That was inappropriate and so uncalled for," she added.

"I probably should have at that point," I consented. "Sure he was rude, abusive and out of line but if that is what it takes for his cat to receive treatment, then so be it. And if he wants to pay me to stand there and listen to his own advice, well then so be it too. I didn't want the cat to die just because its owner is an idiot."

The next morning, however, after a stressful fifteen-hour shift, I wasn't feeling quite so generous when he started again. This time there was no excuse, as he had all night to calm down before deciding how to speak to me, and at this point his cat was out of any immediate danger. We could no longer blame his distress about the situation for his behavior. This time we had only him to blame for his own behavior.

"You shut your mouth and listen to me," he told me for the second time in one evening, only this time via the telephone. This time it was in response to my suggestion that he take his cat to his family veterinarian for continued care, as the cat was still quite ill.

"I'm not transferring him anywhere, he's just fine. You take out that urinary catheter right now and I'll be there to get him." His voice had the 'do-as-you're-told' tone my father used when he was angry.

That was it. I was exhausted enough not to be able to keep my cool. I'd had enough of him in one night. According to hospital policy we are allowed to "fire" clients, particularly if they have a repeat history of abusive or inappropriate behavior. If we choose to do this, we must send them a written letter and offer alternative choices for further veterinary care.

"No, now this time you listen to me," I spat into the receiver through clenched teeth. "If you want to take your cat home that is your prerogative but you need to know the consequences of your decision."

His cat was still really ill and there was a good chance it would die if he took him home. It is fine if an owner wants to take an animal home against medical advice, ultimately any medical decisions they make about their own pets are their legal right to make. What medical care they want is always their choice but, from a legal standpoint, it is my job to make him understand what the consequences of his choices might be for his pet. He quickly cut me off.

"I don't need your medical advice. We're not stupid, maybe your other clients are stupid but my wife and I know all about this stuff. In fact my wife and I probably know more about animals than you do."

Those were actually his words. Imagine that? Apparently this guy has a veterinary degree, and here I thought he never even graduated grade school. This guy was a piece of work. Seething, I hung up the receiver. *Just get down here and pick up your poor cat you ignorant, obnoxious, abusive jerk. This time you have just talked yourself out of ever being allowed into this building again. Take your cat home, if it does live then it is going to have a miserable next few days because of your choices. And you had better hope one of your poor pets never has an emergency again because you are no longer welcome in this building.*

I was curt, yet I remained professional. He wasn't worth losing my job over. I walked down to the manager's office to file the necessary paperwork.

As a veterinarian, all I can do is make recommendations to owners about what kind of care their pet needs. Ultimately it is up to the owner to decide whether or not they will follow those recommendations. Sadly, it is usually the animal that suffers from their choices.

"I think my dog might have eaten mouse bait," a man's voice told me over the phone.

"You should bring him right down," I said, "we'll make him vomit and we'll send you home with the antidote."

Mouse bait is one of my favorite toxicities, if toxins can be favorites for a person. I like this toxicity because it is easily treated if it is addressed in a timely fashion.

"He looks fine, he's bouncing around like nothing has happened," he informed me.

I explained that mouse bait usually takes four to six days before the animal has a problem, and up until then the animal will continue to act normal. This is because rat bait works by inhibiting the animal's ability to clot normally. A week down the line after ingesting the bait, the otherwise healthy animal will start to hemorrhage internally. They arrive at our hospital getting progressively weaker as their lungs or their belly fill with blood. At this point, treatment becomes a much more difficult and expensive undertaking and many of the dogs will die.

"I'll think about it," the man told me, "I'm not even sure if he ate it or not." I could hear voices and loud music in the background.

I tried to convince him that the smartest thing to do was to not take any chances and to come right down for us to initiate treatment. It is better to treat for the possibility of an ingestion than to not treat and be wrong. He agreed but I did not see them at our hospital that evening. Five days later, right on schedule, a young man brought in a white Boxer. A beautiful muscled young dog was lying limp in his arms and breathing heavily.

"He was fine this morning. I found him like this when I got home," the man told me.

I inquired about the dog's history and then started to connect that this was the same person that I had spoken to a few days earlier whose dog may have eaten the rat bait.

The dog's gums were blanched and as white as the man's shirt. The pup's gums were white because he had hemorrhaged into his thorax and had little blood left within his veins. I explained that we needed to start a blood transfusion to replace what he had lost and a plasma transfusion to help his ability to clot. I also explained that he may need a ventilator to breathe if he continued to bleed into his lungs. I created a treatment plan which was well over a thousand dollars. If he needed to be ventilated, that cost would multiply rapidly. If only the man had listened to my advice when this first happened, his dog would be fine and the bill would have been miniscule. On that first evening his treatment would have consisted of getting his dog to vomit, and administering a month's worth of pills. There was no point in would-haves, should-haves, at this point. The man was crying. I'm sure he was feeling guilty about his decision. It's not that he didn't love his dog, he just made a bad choice, a very bad choice. I had a feeling from his responses that he wouldn't be able to help his dog. I wondered if this would be the end for his friend.

Sadly, we see these difficult situations way too frequently in our daily work. Truly we want to help the animal as much as the owner does. We try to convince people to do the right thing but then they don't follow our advice. We want to help but are often unable to. We attempt to treat a severe disease with a method that is highly likely to fail because the owner leaves you with no other options. We sometimes end up euthanizing an innocent animal because his owner has made bad decisions, or euthanizing another because its disease is too much for the owner to handle either mentally, physically, or financially. These scenarios can happen on a daily basis in my line of work, contributing to the syndromes of depression and burnout that are so common in the veterinary profession. As veterinarians, all we can do to ease our own conscience is to care for the animal that we have in front of us to the best of our abilities, and to insure that we have given the owners all available choices. After that, it is out of our hands. The fate of their pet is, and always has been, their choice.

CHAPTER 24

EUTHANASIAS

I am at the doctor's station typing records.

"You have a euthanasia in Room 7," my technician tells me as she is walking by.

Three in the morning is not an uncommon time for euthanasia's if you are in the emergency business. The sound of desperate breathing, or endless pacing during an otherwise quiet night, brings many an owner through our doors in the wee hours of the morning. They are tired of listening to the sounds of their animal's distress, tired of hoping it will be okay until morning. Animals often pick the most inconvenient times to try to die.

"Don't be surprised when you go in there," she adds without further explanation.

I doubt it. At this point in my career, I have seen animals die in every fashion and from every disease imaginable. And each disease seems to have its own mannerism of dying.

Room 7 is the room that our hospital has set up specifically for euthanasia's. For privacy purposes, the room is tucked away in a far corner of the hospital. It contains a couch and carpets in a poorly disguised attempt to remove the clinical atmosphere from the room. I open the door and acquiesce that my technician was right on this one, I am surprised. Shocked, even. In front of me is a scene reminiscent of the aftermath of a violent battle that one sees at the movie theater. The room is empty except for a woman sitting in the center of a room with a large black dog which she is gently rocking in her arms. Giant Schnauzers are an impressive breed…pitch black, statuesque guard dogs weighing up to a hundred pounds. It is a breed that has a pronounced, unwavering, silent stare which has a wilting, unnerving effect when you become the focus of it.

The shocking part for a seasoned veteran of euthanasia's, is the fact that the women and her dog are sitting entwined together in the middle of the room in the midst of a lake of blood. A lake whose shoreline seems to be seeping away from them as I watch. Smears of blood mark the path that they arrived on. The woman's t-shirt is saturated red and she seems oblivious to the red stain growing around her.

She looks up at me tearfully. I can now see the source of the blood. An endless stream is pouring out of her dog's nose as he lays there.

"He has cancer of his nose," she tells me. "We've tried everything from surgery to radiation. The bleeding started up again while he was sleeping and it won't stop. He's ready now and so am I."

Nasal cancers are notorious for invading major blood vessels in the nose. They tend to bleed in large gushers usually for short periods of time, but bleeding of this magnitude I had never seen before. Together, alone in that blood soaked room, we euthanized Simon. And after, we cried together and sat hugging each other silently. I didn't even care that my scrubs were now also soaked with blood.

Crying is rare for me at a euthanasia. I do two to five euthanasia's a day on emergency shifts, sometimes more. I would wither away if I cried at every euthanasia. But the raw vividness of this one strummed cords in my soul that I didn't know were still present. And the woman, Simon's owner, looked so alone and so pathetic in the middle of that large bloody room, holding her giant statuesque dog in her arms.

Euthanasia's are another one of those subjects where I get the old, "I don't know how you do it," response from people.

Again, I don't know how I do it either. You never get used to it. I reconcile it by accepting that I am doing a service to these animals by helping them out of this world peacefully. The alternative usually involves a prolonged slow death for the animals rather than the death most owners hope for, where they die peacefully in their sleep. Unfortunately for all of us, that is not how it usually happens. After a day when I have to euthanize several animals, in order to regain my perspective, I return to my global thinking to keep myself sane. I remind myself again and again that dogs and cats are not an endangered species. They are present in bountiful numbers in the world and many are homeless and starving or in pain. And then I again remind myself there are thousands, if not millions, of adults and children in the world who are poverty stricken, homeless, starving, and ill. This is my coping mechanism for dealing with the endless numbers of euthanasia's and senseless deaths that I have to see or perform on a regular basis. We each have our own ways of coping.

Spend a single day at a local humane shelter and see for yourself how many animals are euthanized each day. I've always thought that every person who chooses to breed their pet, intentionally or not, should spend one day in a humane shelter helping to euthanize the animals who are out of time. That might cure their need to have a litter because it is "such a good dog," or because they want their children to experience the birthing process, or because their pet is papered, or because they want a little extra pocket money. Being sweet or loving or gentle are not good enough reasons to breed a dog. Perhaps witnessing the endless number of animals who are euthanized, many who are registered or papered or who once had loving homes, will cure their need to bring more animals into this over-populated world.

"We'll find the puppies good homes," the owners of a pregnant dog tell me.

I wish they could hear how many other people are telling their veterinarians that all over the country. Each of these litters contribute to the animal overpopulation and a percentage of those well-homed puppies bred around the country end up in a shelter. Breeding should be reserved exclusively for people who care to maintain the health, temperament, and appearance of a certain breed, and who are willing to do the preemptive screenings and provide the necessary care for the dam and puppies.

Euthanasia is one of the only times in a person's life when they are placed in the position of having to choose death for something in their lives that they love. In most cases of illness, we just wait for death to happen. Watching a person or animal die is not necessarily an easier option, depending on how the death occurs.

When to make that decision for their animal is entirely dependent on each person making it. It usually comes down to the "S" word. The "S" word is an expression my first boss liked to use.

"What's that?" I asked the first time he said it to me.

"I don't think they are going to treat their diabetic cat," he told me about a medical case we were both managing, "they are starting to use the S word."

"Suffering," he said. "As soon as they start using the word, suffering, then it's all over."

It didn't take long for me to realize that he was right. As soon as a client starts saying that their pet is suffering it means it's near its demise. I've stopped trying to determine what suffering means to each individual. It's pointless, everyone's concept of the word is different and ultimately it is their own decision to make based on their interpretation of the word, or their interpretation of how it is going to affect their own lives, or how they perceive their animal's condition. Some animals are semi-comatose for weeks and people won't think they are suffering, and other animals will inadvertently urinate on the carpet and owners will chalk it up to 'suffering.'

We all use euphemisms for death. 'Putting them to sleep,' sounds nicer than the word, 'euthanize.' It seems gentler. I was surprised recently by a client who was agonizing over the decision of whether to euthanize her elderly dog. She asked me to explain the process of how we were, "going to put Rosie to sleep?" Rosie was a 15-year-old Brittany Spaniel who had presented to our hospital the night before for sudden onset of violent seizures. Onset of seizures in an older dog is rarely an easily treatable problem and it usually implies a major change which is occurring within their brain such as a rapidly growing tumor. As soon as these words emerged from her mouth, she stopped short and rephrased the sentence to: "I am choosing to kill my dog. How does this process work?"

The bravery of her words struck me. She was one of the few clients I have ever had who decided to face the reality of her pet's death head on.

I still don't understand exactly what happens with death. I'm sure no one does. One minute, an animal is looking at me with doe-like eyes, and then I administer a liquid which is purposefully colored so bright pink that no one will ever mistake it for another drug, and then life seeps out of the animal so rapidly that, even after all of these years, the speed at which that happens continues to surprise me. All that is left in front of me is a cold and still body. Where does that spirit and energy go in those few seconds? One minute it is there, and the next it is gone. And I have the power to do that. I wonder, *why me? Why am I given this power?* Because I have a gilded and sealed piece of paper framed and tacked on a wall with my name on it. *How ridiculous is that?*

"This must be just as hard on you," is the other thing I hear regularly.

Nope, that statement is most certainly not true. This is your beloved pet with whom you have lived for many, many years. This is a dear member of your family. Of course this is harder on you than it is on me. What is hard on me is when people drop their pet off at our hospital to be euthanized because they don't want to be present when it is done. That is the part which is so agonizing for me. The way I see it is that when the owners are present, they are taking responsibility for their pets last moments. When they leave their animal at our hospital, I am the one who becomes responsible for this animal's final moments. Now this poor thing is left in a strange place, frightened and confused, and only has strangers around it during its last moments on earth. Owners drop them off because they don't have the nerve to be there themselves. They can't look their pet in its eyes. I am sympathetic to this sentiment, sometimes people have some really horrific and valid associations with death, yet I still believe that we owe this one small thing to our loyal companions. *Come on,* I want to say to these owners, *stay with your friend just for this moment. Your pet loves you and depends on you and he needs you to comfort him and make him feel safe at this moment.*

We are all a little paranoid that, after we've performed a euthanasia, the animal may not be dead. Euthanasia solution was previously used as an anesthetic solution, so its first effect is to put an animal into a trance-like state that can mimic death. Physicians gave it up as an anesthetic solution when they realized that there was too fine of a line between anesthesia and death when using this drug. There are the odd stories of animals that were euthanized and then found walking around the premises the next day when the staff returned to work. This, thankfully is extremely, extremely rare and probably occurred because an inadequate dose was used. Euthanasia solution is highly effective at doing its job and most veterinarians are diligent about using adequate quantities and insuring that there is no heart beat before they pronounce the pet as dead.

Once I caught one of my colleagues bent over deep into our body freezer with a stethoscope to his ears.

"What are you doing in there?" I asked, not sure I really wanted to hear the answer.

"Don't think I'm weird," he told me with a sheepish grin on his face, "I just wanted to confirm this pet was dead. I was distracted with an emergency after I euthanized him and never confirmed it."

"Of course I don't think you're weird, Charlie," I replied with a purposefully incredulous tone, "it's perfectly normal to be listening to frozen bodies in the freezer."

I smiled to myself, I knew Charlie wasn't weird. This was just a weird profession.

Most people are curious about what happens to their pet after it is euthanized. Many people have expressed their concern that their animal, or its body, may be used for medical research. I can honestly say that in all my years of being a vet, and in all the practices I have worked at, I have never seen anyone do anything unethical to an animal after it is deceased. Most veterinary staff and crematorium staffs treat the animal's bodies with only the utmost respect. And every crematorium that I have worked with has been pristine about insuring that the correct ashes are returned to the correct owners.

One beautiful young Rottweiler I took care of all weekend had severe and widespread disease of her lungs. The dog spent the whole weekend on my ER shifts, dependent on oxygen to breathe and trying to recover from her disease. Her family was so committed to her. They had driven four hours in the middle of the night to seek help. Unfortunately, her disease was too widespread by the time we started to work with her. She spent both days struggling to breathe, which was excruciating for everyone to watch but, because she was young and had a chance of surviving, her owners wanted us to continue trying. Early Monday morning I realized she was getting rapidly worse. I called them to let them know I thought this might be her last minutes. Thankfully they had visited her earlier that evening and had been able to spend some quality time with her. They rushed down to our hospital to be with her.

"Hold on baby, hold on. You have to keep living," they told her, hugging her closely as she gasped for air.

"We went too far with our other dog," the man said to me a few minutes later. "I don't want to do the same with her."

My technicians and I looked at each other and exchanged incredulous glances. I knew we were all thinking the same thing. How much farther could you possibly go than this? This dog had been struggling to breathe all weekend. Yet they still couldn't make that final call.

Making that decision of when to euthanize your pet is incredibly difficult. Trying to predict when an animal is going to die is challenging even for veterinary professionals. As veterinarians, we try to guide people in making those choices, but it is not always obvious to us either when those last minutes will be. There is an old adage which says it is better to euthanize an animal a week too early than an hour too late. I think that is a wise saying that we should all take note of. No one wants to find themselves in a sterile hospital environment with their dying pet in the middle of the night because they could not make the decision earlier.

Later on in my career, I started doing euthanasia's at people's homes. I wanted to give people the choice of having a gentle goodbye with their pet in the privacy and familiarity of their own home. I learned through harsh experiences, how important it was for owners to have the choice to be able to say goodbye to their pet somewhere, anywhere other than an unfamiliar hospital environment. Most veterinary professionals would never consider euthanizing their animal at the hospital so why shouldn't pet owners of the world have that same option. What I didn't expect when I started this service, was how much more difficult a euthanasia at the home setting would be for me. By arriving at their homes, I was suddenly immersed in the lives of these people and their pets. I was seeing where that pet lived and played, its favorite toys, its animal companions, and the children of the home. The euthanasia's simultaneously became much easier and more personal for the animal, and more agonizing to me. Still, I never regretted starting that service. Allowing the animal to be at home during its last moments meant so much to the owners, and so much to the animals, who could gently fall asleep in their own bed and in the comfort and privacy of their own home.

CHAPTER 25

EDNA, I THINK

People choose to pay for an animal's medical care for some very odd reasons. Guilt is a powerful motivator. I was surprised one day to walk into an exam room to find a backyard chicken sitting on the exam table.

"This is Edna," the finely dressed couple who were accompanying the chicken told me. "But it could be Olga or Mary, we're not actually sure. We're taking care of our brother's house and all of their critters. Our dog attacked their chickens."

For the purposes of the day, we decided to call this chicken, Edna. Edna was a fine specimen. She was a large and well-muscled chicken and had shiny red and black feathers. Exuding a mannerism of self-importance, Edna held her head high and surveyed the room from her perch on the exam table. The man pulled back a swath of feathers to show me a large laceration in the muscles that were directly behind her right wing. Edna seemed unhappy that I was inspecting her without permission. She responded to my exam with a loud series of reprimanding clucks. The wound was quite deep and exposed the underlying bone and tendons. The skin surrounding the wound was macerated and raw from the dog's teeth.

I added up the costs of her care at our emergency hospital. Between the exam, the anesthesia, the surgical time, the surgical supplies, and the postoperative medications, the bill came to over $400. At that cost, I doubted that they would authorize her treatment. I didn't want to see Edna end up on the butcher table because of an exuberant, loose dog. I removed the exam fee and discounted a few items to reduce the total. As I did not own the hospital, I could discount my own services and time, but not the supply costs or technician time involved.

"I can fix her for $240," I told them hesitantly. I wondered if this was going to be the end of Edna.

The husband and wife exchanged glances. "It was our fault," the wife said, "and it is your brother's prize chickens." Reluctantly they agreed to Edna's surgery.

When I took Edna into the back, the technicians laughed. "Do they know chicken breast is $2.99 a pound at the grocery store?" they asked.

Edna who weighed in at about four pounds did not seem to find this funny at all.

Edna, being the elegant lady chicken that she was, did not fight us as we anesthetized her. We plucked her feathers to create a cleaner wound and then I carefully closed up her laceration. I was pleased with the final outcome and felt that it would heal up nicely. When I was done, I gently rolled the still-sleeping-Edna over so she would wake up in a nesting position. As I turned her over, a large brown egg rolled out from beneath her belly.

"An egg, an egg," I announced gleefully, holding it up for everyone in the room to see. I could not ever remember having a patient who produced an egg for me while I was caring for it.

"No way Edna," I said, placing the still groggy chicken's beak close to my face, "listen up, even if you are Olga or Mary. This is not the depression era. I do not take eggs in exchange for my services. You can pay in the traditional manner, just like every other pet that walks through this door."

Edna was unimpressed. With matronly dignity she settled herself on top of her perfect egg. She knew the value of her produce and nobody was going to tell this dignified hen otherwise.

210

The next owner and pet that arrived did not have such a happy ending. ER shifts are always like that. Stretches of happy, treatable cases intermixed with sad situations. The young girl in the exam room was hugging an adorable Pekingese-poodle mix close to her body. It was the cutest little dog that I'd seen in months. I could only see Twinky's right side but when her owner placed her on the table the image in front of me suddenly looked like an advertisement for a B-rated horror flick.

Twinky's left eye was popped out. The eye stuck out three inches forward from the socket and was veering off oddly to one side. Drips of blood were trickling down her face. If Twinky had been a puppet, there would be a vibrating spring behind the protruding eye. Perhaps equally as disturbing, I was unperturbed by this gruesome sight. That's because I had seen it many times before. It's the owners that you have to calm down and attempt to console. Their reaction is usually much more animated than mine. An eye which has been traumatically disengaged from the eye socket is called a proptoses in veterinary medicine. It usually occurs from a blunt force trauma to the head region or from violent shaking and is most common in smush-faced breeds, such as Shih Tzus, Pugs, and Boston terriers, who also have shallow eye sockets.

"I took her for a walk. She was on a leash. This large Labrador came running across the lawn and grabbed her in its mouth."

The girl was obviously shaken up by the events of the afternoon. She lived in an apartment complex filled with students. Dogs were often seen running loose, which was against apartment regulations. She had taken her young dog outside to go potty and its life had been violently altered because an owner had failed to keep his dog on a leash.

I moistened the dry eye and administered pain medications to Twinky. Sometimes a proptosed eye can be saved but the fact that Twinky's traumatized eye was veering off to one side told me that significant muscle damage had occurred and, along with that, the pupil was dilated. Both of these are bad prognostic signs, the latter telling me that the optic nerve had been damaged. Based on the degree of damage that had been incurred, it was unlikely that the dog would have vision in this eye, and a good chance that the eye itself could not be saved. I gave the owner her options. We could try to save the eye, but the odds were high that it would not work. If the eye did not survive, Twinky would need a second surgery down the line to remove the eye.

"No just take it out," the girl told me sadly. "It doesn't sound good and I don't want to traumatize her by going through all these medical procedures. She is a really good dog and she does not deserve this." She signed the permission forms authorizing me to surgically remove her dog's eye. I thought it was a good decision.

"Are the owners of the Labrador paying?" I asked.

"You're damn right they are," she said.

It was a small and unsatisfying compensation for the loss of her dog's eye. I didn't tell her, but from past experiences, I knew that it was unlikely that she would ever collect a cent from the negligent owners. Police officers and animal control officers are notorious for being of little help in these situations. They have too many other important things to worry about, and a dog losing its eye is not one of them.

CHAPTER 26

THE MISADVENTURES OF DORIS

I tend to be extremely picky about the animals I bring into my life. At work one night, a young woman and her two children arrived at our hospital with a miniature poodle with a broken leg. The poodle had an obvious fracture of her hind leg, which had occurred in their back yard. Despite her injury, the tiny poodle was darting and bouncing her way around the exam room, wagging her tail and offering kisses at every opportunity she could. It took three of us to catch her as she ran wildly around the back of the hospital, fearlessly charging into each room with her leg in the air..

When I put her in a cage, she lifted her broken hind leg straight up in the air and supported it with the back of her head as if to say, "It's broken, it's broken. Hello. Hello. It's this leg. "

It was as if she couldn't figure out what else to do with the useless leg. She spent the night in that awkward and very goofy position. It should have been a warning as to what I had in front of me.

I was so enamored by her silly exuberance, that after x-raying and splinting the leg, I heard myself say, "Let me know if you ever want to get rid of her," to the owner. I quickly wondered what had possessed me to say that as generally I make it a rule not to adopt animals that come into the clinic.

The next day, sure enough, I got a call from the owner. "Did you really mean that about taking her?" she asked.

The woman explained that she was going through a divorce, recently had spinal surgery, and had a sick parent and two young children to care for.

"I just don't have the time or the resources to take care of her with a broken leg," she told me.

I thought about it, wondering if I was insane to take a young poodle puppy, and then agreed to take her. Poodles are a breed that had always entranced me. I like their intelligence, energy, independence and lack of shedding. The exchange of the puppy took place in the parking lot of Walmart. What struck me as odd about the whole deal, in addition to the fact that we were doing this in a Walmart parking lot, was how emotionless everyone was. The two children, about eight and twelve in age, calmly handed her over to me in her crate and not one of them shed a tear or even said goodbye to her. *That's odd*, I thought, *there doesn't seem to be much love in this household.* The puppy immediately bounded into my arms, smothering me with kisses, showing as equal concern about leaving her old family as they had shown about leaving her with me. *This darling pup at least deserves a household who loves her,* I thought to myself.

I renamed her Doris. It seemed an appropriate name for a poodle, a dog usually associated with being a grandma type of dog. I had her leg repaired. It did not take me long to realize that, not only was this puppy absolutely insane, but she was suicidal as well. After mysteriously breaking her leg in her own back yard, she managed to fall into our front pond twice, once immediately after I had changed her time-consuming splint. Later she barely missed electrocuting herself when I found her chewing through my blow dryer's cord as I dried my hair. And then there was the fentanyl incident.

After her surgery she had a fentanyl patch placed on her hind leg. The patch slowly leaks a potent morphine-like substance into the body and avoids the need of having to give pain medications by mouth. After three days I removed the patch and carefully threw it away. I placed Doris into her crate and went upstairs to pack for our camping trip. When I returned downstairs, I remarked about how quiet Doris was being, a rare event for her. When I went to move her crate, I realized she was being way too good and way too quiet. I pulled her out of the crate and found myself holding a limp and lifeless dog in my arms. Her gums were white and her heart rate was extremely slow at thirty-six. *What the hell?* I panicked. *What could have happened?* I knew that I had thrown the patch away so she could not have ingested it, and ten minutes ago she was bouncing out of control in her usual ridiculous poodle fashion. Maybe she was bleeding out from her fracture site. I called down to the ER hospital where I worked and told them I was coming down with my puppy, whom I thought was dying.

"Say goodbye to her honey," I yelled, as I ran out the door.

The way she was looking, I was truly frightened that this might be a final goodbye. Whatever had happened, something was terribly wrong with Doris.

In the car, I held the lifeless little figure on my lap. "Doris, Doris," I yelled.

Doris lifted up her head, rolled her eyes backward, rolled her head and then sunk back down.

"Doris. Wake Up. Keep fighting."

I was gently shaking her and trying to keep her conscious as we drove. Her heart rate would momentarily speed up and then her eyes would roll down beneath her lower lids again. It was then that I realized she was acting like she was anesthetized. It must have been the fentanyl patch, but I knew that I had thrown it away and she had not chewed on it. So how could that be? I hypothesized that maybe she licked the glue remnants from the fentanyl patch after I had pulled it off and got an overdose of the drug from that. Unlikely, but possible. Just knowing what might be happening to my puppy made me feel a bit better about her condition. I could deal with anesthetized.

When I got to the hospital, our criticalist was there with all the emergency supplies laid out in front of her. We got an IV line in and tried the opioid-reversing drug called naloxone. Before you could blink, my listless puppy was bouncing and leaping in the arms of our technician, Emily, who was frantically and unsuccessfully trying to restrain her. I breathed a sigh of relief, knowing that it was something treatable. Great, not only do I have a crazy, suicidal puppy but she appears to be a junkie as well. *You're killing me Doris, and I've only owned you about seven days.* I left Doris at the hospital for the doctors to monitor for more signs of an overdose and went off on my camping trip.

The last straw came when I sent Doris home with one of our technicians for a 'sleepover.' She would often go over to this maternally stern technician's house and play with her and her dog, Katie. Doris loved sleepover camp, and I loved it because Doris was entertained and came home exhausted. This also meant she would sleep the day away with me when I worked the overnights, instead of intermittently jumping on my head just for the fun of it. On this particular evening, Doris left to go home with the technician at 6:00 and returned to the hospital at about 10:00 with her face and neck covered in blood.

"What happened?" I inquired, surveying my now red, discolored poodle who was still bouncing around the room.

"It was a freak accident," drawled the Southern-accented technician. "Her lower eyelid became pierced by the S-hook of Katie's rabies tag. They both became frightened and Katie ran off around the yard, dragging Doris behind her with Doris's eyelid still attached to her collar. We finally were able to stop them and had to cut the hook to detach them."

In all my years as a veterinarian, I had never heard of one dog becoming attached to another dog by its rabies tag piercing through its eyelid, and then being dragged around the yard in this manner. Only Doris. The next day, I requested that Doris be placed on the pet insurance plan. This one needed it. I could not afford not to.

Later on, for kicks and giggles, I decided to give Doris a Mohawk and color it pink. It seemed that I had the world's most ridiculous dog and I wanted a haircut that reflected that personality. Plus, she wasn't a sissy, she was tough. The Mohawk was a hit with nearly everyone. Generally, people would laugh when they saw it.

"Nice doo, doggy," I would get when we walked down the streets, or pulled up at the McDonalds drive-through.

Everyone had an opinion on her Mohawk, and an opinion on the color when I chose to change it. Pink is not her color, or the purple makes her look too "bad ass," or the orange makes her look like a "pee-head" or "Big Bird."

Doris seemed not to mind and continued to remain her exuberant, goofy self despite the current color of her Mohawk. Later we even found a groomer who was willing to make it striped. She told me she had to place foil in Doris' hair so the colors wouldn't bleed. I admit that I am a bit reluctant to reveal the fact that my dog goes to the groomer and her hair is done with foil, as I don't want my professional reputation tarnished.

Some people seemed to take real offense at Doris' Mohawk. One day I was peacefully walking down the street with her when a man and his hunting dog passed us by.

The man turned around, looked at Doris and asked me, "Did you dye her hair?"

"Yeah," I smiled.

"Get a life!" he yelled loudly at me over his shoulder.

I was a little taken aback, then angry, and then I decided to ignore him.

Okay, I'll do that, I thought to myself, *I'll go get a life.*

The man took a few more steps and then turned around again.

"Get a real dog!" he yelled.

That was it. The New Yorker in me flared out.

"She is a real dog," I snapped back. "Spend twenty-four hours with her and you'll be overwhelmed by her real dogginess."

"We told him," I whispered to Doris, "don't you pay any attention to that nasty old unhappy man." We continued on with our walk. Doris didn't care and marched on, taking on the world as she did in every one of our walks.

I get a certain amount of flak for the fact that I own a dog with colored hair. But I'm beyond caring about what other people's opinions are about this subject. I see so much suffering and misery in animals on a daily basis that being light hearted and having fun with my own dog seems quite harmless in the grand scheme of things. Besides, Doris owns that Mohawk image more than any dog I've ever owned. I joke with people that she is one of the few poodles who emerged from the womb sporting a colored Mohawk on her head.

The truth of the matter is that Doris was one of the toughest and most athletic dogs I've ever known. There would be no lounging on the couch or pampered prissy playing for this eight-pound poodle. This toy poodle was a tom-girl. She loved rolling in the dirt, playing in the rain, bossing around the big farm dogs, and darting into the pastures to eat horse manure. She would go on strenuous backpacking trips with us. She hiked to the top of several large mountains, scampering up steep rocky slopes like a mountain goat. She survived several frightening thunder and hail storms in the mountains with little anxiety. She went on a long white-water adventure with us in the boat. There was nothing wimpy about her. This was not a toy dog who was going to cling to the skirts of her owners. Instead, she would drag us along on field trips to the local stores and greet people with enthusiasm.

Ben liked to take her to the local Home Depot for supply trips. He would walk into the store with a poodle sporting her colored Mohawk and sweater that he had put on her himself.

"Don't you wonder that they'll think you're a fairy?" I laughingly asked of him.

Ben is one of those ridiculous men who is afraid to accompany my friends and me when we go to gay bars dancing, out of fear that he'll be hit on.

"Not really," he answered.

"You're walking into a man's hardware store with a poodle who is sporting a Mohawk and wearing a pink sweater and you don't think people will wonder if you're gay?" I inquired again.

"I don't care," he replied, really meaning it. He paused and then added, "I love her and we have a lot of fun together."

That was the end of the conversation. In his mind, those words should explain everything. I smiled to myself, watching him curled up on the couch with the little Mohawked poodle fast asleep on his lap and I was reminded, once again, of why I love him so much.

CHAPTER 27

CARING

received an email from the hospital manager that a client had written a complaint about me. I had treated her dog the previous week on an emergency visit. The dog had sustained a scratch to the surface of his eye. A corneal scratch is quite painful and the dog had been holding his swollen eye shut, obviously in severe discomfort. I took the time to show the owner how to properly apply the eye medication so it would be effective. I also discussed, in depth, how to administer the oral pain medications, and I discussed the side effects that could potentially result from their use. In between trying to help her, I kept popping into exam room 3 next door, to check on an elderly man whose schnauzer had just been killed by a passing car. His dog had escaped out of his front yard when a delivery man opened the gate. The little dog was the only living creature in his home, as he had recently lost his wife. His grief was palpable by the silence in the room and the tears that welled out of his eyes as he clutched the cold body of his little friend to his chest.

The owner of the dog with the scratched eye seemed to be happy until she received the bill at check out. At that time, she became unexpectedly angry. People's dissatisfaction with veterinary care is often centered around the money that they have to spend on the treatment. Her formal complaint, which came in a letter, also requested a refund for the money she had spent. One of her reasons was that she had waited too long in the ER waiting room.

"What kind of an incompetent emergency room makes an emergency wait two hours? And the vet was only in there for ten minutes at best." She added that she did not feel that the veterinarian cared about her dog. This was the part of her complaint that really offended me. Being told that you don't care as a medical professional is a very personal comment...about as offensive as being called greedy if you were the director of a charity organization.

The truth is that I did care that her dog was in discomfort. I cared very much. If I didn't care, I would not have bothered to dispense pain medications, nor would I have taken the time to personally show her how to medicate the eye. Practicing good quality medicine, and offering the best possible treatment to obtain a successful outcome for every animal that I see, is my way of caring. And because I am able to diagnose and treat an animal in an effective and efficient manner is one of the reasons that she did not have to wait longer than two hours for me to see her pet who had a non-critical condition. And lastly, if I emoted for every animal and every client that I saw, I think I would end up hospitalized myself.

That night I vented to my Ben, my long term partner. "I see thirty sick animals and sixty family members each day. I see many different degrees of suffering, some minor and some excruciating. Owners don't have that realm of experience. Some think that every time their pet whines, it is in major distress. Maybe I don't emote sadness and compassion with every room that I see but, realistically, how is a person expected to do that? Maybe I have stopped caring."

Caring is a funny thing. As a veterinarian, you are involved with heartwrenching situations on a regular basis. You have to have the capacity to deal with seeing animals in pain, and seeing their owners in pain but, equally as important, you are expected, in this profession, to have the capacity to convey that you don't care. Some people can't afford medical care. Some people don't think a pet is worth spending that kind of money on. Some people truly don't have compassion or concern for an animal's welfare. Some people can't manage the aftercare and some people don't want their animal to suffer – whatever suffering may mean to that person at that moment. In these situation, you have to have the capacity to mask any feelings you might have when a person chooses not to treat their animal's disease or discomfort.

Regardless of the reason why owners choose not to treat, it is my obligation to nod my head with a gracious smile and verbally reaffirm that I understand why they are unable to have their elderly cat's fractured leg repaired. And then, I find myself pushing the euthanasia solution into a beautiful animal, who is looking up at me with trusting eyes, because this is the outcome that the owners have chosen for it. As a professional, I am expected to quietly accept their decision and later console their grief, and then I am expected to help them justify the choice they have made. After it is done, I have to justify my own actions to myself over and over again.

It's not just me feeling this way, I realized one day when one of our managers in a particularly frustrated moment blurted out, "I swear you have to be schizophrenic to do this job. One moment I have to show sadness and empathy to an owner for some sad situation that has happened to their pet, and the next I'm supposed to smile and cater to some crazy, nasty person who doesn't think I'm putting her medications up quick enough. It's maddening." She finished wiping away the rare tear that I've ever seen from her.

At home on TV, I watch the video footage of young soldiers who were killed in the war, or I watch a tsunami sweep over and destroy thousands of homes and lives. I am once again reminded, with a sickening clarity, of all the injustices that occur every day and every minute in this world. And then in some sick way, I feel a bit better about all the needless euthanasia's that I am forced to perform. In the grand scheme of things, I have to remember that the beautiful animal is after all just a cat. And I have to remember that cats and dogs are overpopulated and that shelters kill hundreds every day.

And that is what becomes the real struggle and test over time...whether each of us as veterinarians have the capacity and strength, year after year, to emote in one situation, but not in the next. To treat an animal who has minor pain with the same level of caring and concern as a critical patient because that's what an owner wants from us. To understand and truly emphasize with every owner when they choose not to treat their animal or when they choose to neglect their animal's medical problems.

My emotions went from self-contemplation to irritation as I started thinking about this woman's complaint. What right does she have to pass judgment on me? What does she know about me and my life? How many times has she dealt with life and death situations and how many times, if ever, has she had to be the initiator of ending a living being's life? This is a never ending task that I sometimes do multiple times in a day. How would that affect her ability to express caring and concern over time? Would she feel any differently if she knew I was simultaneously helping an elderly man in the next room who's long term canine companion had just been violently killed by a passing car? Would that be caring enough for her? Would she realize even then that her dog's medical problem and temporary pain was minor in the grand scheme of things?

"Sweets, you do care," Ben replied patiently, putting his arm around me to comfort me. "It is obvious that you care by how you come home every day, worried about every patient that you treated. You agonize over cases, spend hours reading journals to improve yourself, and have restless, sleepless nights. Nobody is superhuman, and the ones that overly emote are probably faking it."

I contemplated his words. I knew he was right, I had never stopped caring about my patients. Yet, if I was really being honest with myself, I had to admit that there was an element of truth to this woman's accusation. Over the years, little by little, I had stopped trying to connect with every owner that I saw. It was an act of self-preservation. I no longer had the energy to help every anxious, stressed out owner that walked through the door. And to the client, that probably translated as not caring about their pet. Maybe this was a form of burnout.

It has come to light in recent years that my profession is in trouble. A recent study, performed in Britain, found that veterinarians are four times more likely to commit suicide than the average person, and two times more likely to commit suicide than our counterparts in the healthcare profession. As a profession, we have achieved the ignominy of replacing the dental profession as having the highest suicide rate. It is not a statistic to be proud of. The frightening results of this study shook my profession wide awake. The simultaneous suicides of two high-profile veterinarians in the United States brought the reality of the problem home once again. These suicides became the initiators in instigating public conversations amongst the veterinary community that obviously should have happened long ago. Articles and blogs about depression and suicide started to appear more frequently in journals and in on-line formats. I was so glad that this issue had finally begun to gain attention and that my profession had begun to publicly acknowledge this very sad trend. As all participants in an Alcoholics Anonymous program know, the first step to fixing a problem is to acknowledge that there is a problem.

The high rate of suicide in the profession is attributed to a variety of factors. Veterinarians work excessively long hours, often have clients with excessive expectations, and we deal with life and death situations on a daily basis. We graduate with huge education loans and have half the financial earning capacity of physicians. Veterinarians tend to be pleasers and if we cannot meet a client's expectations, or the outcome of a case is negative, we are prone to feelings of inadequacy or self-beratement. The nature of our work makes us highly susceptible to burnout and compassion fatigue. Also as a group, our personalities tend to be conscientious and sensitive. We also tend to be high achievers and highly driven perfectionists. We often have quirky personality traits that may isolate us from the norm. All of these traits are known factors in increasing suicidal tendencies. Many of us work solo and in isolated situations, and have few people to confer with about potentially life-altering decisions for our patients. Perhaps, most importantly, we are experts in the concept of inducing death and our perspective about euthanasia tends to be different than that of the average person. Euthanasia is a practice which is seen in a positive light amongst veterinarians and euthanasia is a choice that we can offer as a means of providing a peaceful death to a critically ill or traumatized animal.

We have plenty of access to powerful, lethal drugs and, of course, we are experts in how to administer them. In one study, more than fifty percent of the veterinarians who committed suicide used the euthanasia solutions that they had available in their clinics to end their life. Another study showed that self-poisoning with drugs, most often the barbiturates commonly found on the shelves of a veterinary hospital, accounted for 76 to 89 percent of suicides in veterinarians. This is compared to the general public, who uses medications only 20 to 46 percent of the time to end their lives. I find it interesting, in a very sad way, that the percentage of suicide attempts is much lower than that of the general public, even though the suicide rate itself is much higher. The operative word in the sentence being 'attempts.' This is because, as a group who are high achievers and perfectionists, and who have free access to the most lethal of drugs, we tend to be more successful than the general public in achieving the desired result.

Clearly, the people in my profession do care. The biggest problem amongst my colleagues seems to be that, as professionals, we care just a little too much. And it is now clear, that as a whole community, we need to learn to care for ourselves just a little bit better.

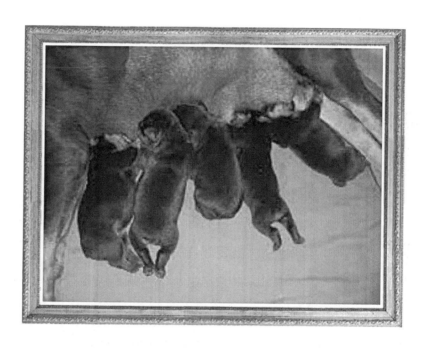

CHAPTER 28

A TAIL'S END

This chapter's title references tails so, of course, some veterinary stories about tails seem to be in order. Where shall we start? Tail dockings are one of the things that I dislike the most as a vet. Certain breeds such as Rottweilers, Dobermans, boxers, and poodles are expected to have their tails surgically shortened to comply with AKC breed standards. There is a never ending debate amongst veterinary professionals as to whether the practices of ear cropping and tail docking are ethical, as these procedures cause pain and disfigurement to an animal. Yet, most people who own a specific breed want them to look a precise way. Somehow a Doberman with a long tail and floppy ears just doesn't look like the fierce guard dog it is supposed to be. And breeders are aware that a dog who is not cropped would never succeed in the show ring, or be accepted by the average buyer.

Traditionally, puppy's tails are docked before they are five days of age. The tail is excised without anesthesia. The theory is that pain sensation is not highly developed at this age. It is also because vets are, rightfully, very tentative about anesthetizing such a frail neonate. When I am presented with a box of tiny, snuggling puppies whose owners want their tails docked, I look at them sleeping peacefully and I am aware of the melee and bloodshed that is to come when we start the procedure. The technician will hold the tiny creature upside down as I tie a small tourniquet around the base of its tail. Using a scalpel, I will incise first through the skin, and then between the vertebrae, and then through the spinal cord at the level of the tail that the breed standard dictates. We all have charts for the proper length we are to cut off of the tail when a tail docking is requested. The puppy, who is supposed to not feel pain, is screaming bloody murder the whole time, and writhing to get away from us. Almost invariably, it urinates and defecates while I perform the procedure...reason enough to believe it must be feeling something. The other pups who were sleeping soundly, awaken and start vocalizing just as loud, sensing that there is a problem with one of their siblings.

The American Kennel Club's official position on tail and ear docking is that they "recognize that ear cropping, tail docking, and dewclaw removal, as described in certain breed standards, are acceptable practices integral to defining and preserving breed character and/or enhancing good health. Appropriate veterinary care should be provided."

Well appropriate veterinary care is me, and I don't like the practice one bit. I hate torturing animals just to define a standard that the human race finds appealing. Each time I went to perform tail dockings, I had to steel myself mentally to do it. I continued to do it as a service because many clients want it, breed standards still dictate it, and because I have seen the ramifications of home ear croppings and tail dockings. Yet another perk of being an ER veterinarian is that tail dockings and ear croppings are never requested of me.

Tails serve a multitude of functions and are a body part unique to the animal world. Tails serve as a balancing tool, allowing squirrels to agilely run along a power line. They offer a way to express emotions, as in a cat who swishes its tail to show its anger. A dog can show signs of pleasure or excitement by exuberantly wagging its tail. They also serve as weapons, as in a kimono dragon who uses its tail to maim its prey. A tail can be a means to anchor oneself, as in a monkey swinging from limb to limb. It can be an extra leg for a kangaroo who wants to stand up taller. The tail becomes a signaling device when a hunting dog erects it upon finding a bird. Fish use it to propel themselves forward and to steer themselves. It fine tunes steering and flight in a bird. Human fetuses in the womb begin with a tail that regresses before they are born. This fact has been used as an argument to support the theory of evolution.

"Do you have any stories about tails?" I ask Cowboy Pete, a man we were chatting with while sitting at a bar on top of a mountain pass in Montana. We had stopped there waiting for a snow storm to subside.

"Oh sure," he drawled slowly, "I had a horse that we left in a pasture one night and when I returned in the morning he had no tail. Turns out the goat in the next pasture spent the whole night grazing on it."

I tried to picture this event and then started to wonder if he was spinning me a tall tale himself. Goats don't eat horse's tails. Or do they?

"Or how about those cows whose tails just fall off?" He went on spitting a clump of tobacco into a cup on the bar. This guy must be spinning tall tales, I decided. I didn't remember learning about a mysterious tail-falling-off disease in vet school.

"Why would that happen?" I questioned him dubiously.

"It's those cow dogs. They get a little rough sometimes, just can't help themselves. They run after the cows and try to herd them, then they grab their tail and hang onto 'em. A few weeks later when that area rots, the tail just falls off."

It actually made sense, similar types of injuries will happen to cats that have trauma to their tails. Ranching stories always fascinate me, as it is such a far reality from my own daily life. Ranchers and owners are often wiser than what we give them credit for. After all, they are the ones living with their creatures day in and day out, and they know all the strange nuances of animal's health that we are never taught in vet school.

Mind you, I could tell him a tale or two of my own about tails after having lived a few years in this profession. I could tell him about the cat who got his tail caught in the electric garage door and hung there for several hours before the owners found him. I could tell him about the teenager who accidentally cut off his Labrador's tail with a sickle on

Christmas Eve while weed-wacking. The boy came in to my New England hospital with tears in his eyes, holding up his dog's amputated segment of tail. He wanted to know if I could reattach it. *Nope, not possible, but Merry Christmas anyway.*

I remembered all of the cats that came in with large swellings at the base of their tails where an abscess has formed. This usually happens several days after having been bit by another cat. You can always tell the fraidy cats from the instigating cats. The passive cats have bite marks on the back ends of their bodies as they are running away from the aggressive encounters, while the scrappy fighters have lashes around their ears and eyes as they take on an opponent, head first.

And then there are the dogs that develop cuts on the tip of their tails. They walk around wagging their tail, leaving blood splatters throughout the walls until their homes begin to mimic a great Jackson Pollock painting. Just as the tail tip starts to heal, the exuberant dog will whack it again which restarts the bloodshed and mess. This cycle sometimes goes on for days until, finally, the frustrated owner arrives at our hospital, looking for help with what should be a very minor problem.

If you listened to the various tales of veterinarians of the world, which includes small animal vets, equine vets, swine vets, zoo vets, and game park vets, you would most likely be astounded. You would hear about vets repairing the broken shell of a giant tortoise, vets placing a peg leg on a pony, vets removing a stake from the chest of a dog who impaled itself, vets performing a C-section on a cow on a cold winter night, vets repairing a wound on the neck of a giraffe, or vets treating a litter of snow leopards with eye infections. Veterinarian's real life stories read like storybook tall tales, yet their stories are unexaggerated.

I am proud of my profession. We are doing our best, in a difficult and emotional field, to help the numerous species of animals in the world, in a multitude of fashions. And even to this day, after so many years of seeing both the positive and negatives of the profession, I still think it is a very worthwhile pursuit. I try to encourage young people, who express an interest in the profession, to follow that dream if that is truly what they want. I can't imagine a more rewarding career, and I don't know of a profession which requires a more diverse set of skills and knowledge. There is not a day at work where I don't see something new, see a new variation of the old, or learn something that I did not know before. It is a fascinating and ever evolving profession.

Every day we are honored by being brought into the dynamics and emotions of a family, and this allows us to help people when they are most vulnerable. We are a caring and kind group of people who will often go to extremes to help our clients and their pets. Of course, as in any profession, there is room to improve but the industry is gradually making changes and most veterinarians that I know strive to practice quality and conscientious medicine. I have never doubted, even for a minute, my own choice to become a veterinarian. The journey through both my career and personal life has been a windy path, as is true for many people, but ultimately I ended up exactly where I was supposed to be. Right here.

There is a quote that I like, by author Julia Glass, which states: *"When it comes to life, we spin our own yarn, and where we end up is really, in fact, where we always intended to be."* The idea that we have all spun our own life's tales is thought-provoking and perhaps frustrating, but I like the idea that even seemingly bad choices are merely changes in direction that will still leave us walking on the correct path. The journey that I have taken through my own career and personal life has been a windy path, and my ball of yarn is kinked, frayed, and filled with knots, but at least I know that I ended up exactly where I was supposed to be. Which is right here, who I am now, and where I am now... an emergency veterinarian with a hell of a lot of good stories to tell.

And I will let that notion be the tail end of this veterinarian's tale.

Made in the USA
San Bernardino, CA
17 July 2017